Tapping Student Effort

Increasing Student Achievement

Also by Stephen G. Barkley:

Quality Teaching in a Culture of Coaching

Wow! Adding Pizzazz to Teaching and Learning

Tapping Student Effort

Increasing Student Achievement

By Stephen G. Barkley

with Contributing Editor Terri Bianco

PERFORMANCE
LEARNING SYSTEMS.

Performance Learning Systems, Inc.®

Publications Division

Performance Learning Systems, Inc.® Publications Division
© 2007 Performance Learning Systems, Inc.
All Rights Reserved.
Printed in the United States of America
10 9 8 7 6 5 4 3

PLS® Products
72 Lone Oak Drive
Cadiz, KY 42211
800-506-9996
Fax 270-522-2014
http://www.plsweb.com/resources/products/books/effort

Library of Congress Cataloging-to-Publication Data

Barkley, Stephen G. (Stephen George), 1950-
  Tapping student effort, increasing student achievemment / by Stephen G.
  Barkley; with contributing editor Terri Bianco.
     p. cm.
  Includes bibliographical references and index.
  ISBN-13: 978-1-892334-23-7 (pbk. : alk. paper)
  ISBN-10: 1-892334-23-2 (pbk. : alk. paper)
  1. Motivation in eduucation. 2. Effective Teaching. 3. Academic
I. Bianco, Terri. II. Title.

LB1065.B374 2007
370.15'4–dc22
                              2006028555

Cover Design & Internal Design: Shari A. Resinger, Art Director
Index: Brackney Indexing Service
Adobe Fonts: ITC Cheltenham and Cosmos

Dedication

*This book is dedicated to
my mother Helen Duh Barkley and to
my daughter Shannan Barkley Biddelman.
They both taught me much about effort
in learning, living, and loving*

Contents

Acknowledgments

I would like to express my sincere appreciation and admiration to the team that helped develop this book and to the educators throughout the country who have tapped their students' effort, leading to increased achievement.

The following educators have shared with me their exceptional ideas which have made this book possible, and I thank them all: Sarah Lovelidge, North Bend Elementary, Harford County, MD with story her about Bradley; Chick Moorman, of Personal Power Press with his story about Skywalker Sprouts (from his newsletter and Website); David Bordenkircher, Principal, South Lake High School, Lake County, FL for recounting his days as a band leader; John Schmitt, Advanced Placement and Honors Psychology instructor, McDowell High School, Erie, PA for his information on test taking and the story of Andy; Penny Jadwin, Professional Development Specialist, Lynn Haven, FL for her story about Antoinette;

Diane Moeller, Principal, Kennedy Elementary, St. Joseph, MN with her stories about Mary and the banana split; Mark Thompson, Director, National Educator Program, Tampa, FL for his contribution about teachers who recall projects that require hard work; and to Barbara Carroll and Karen Bailin, Cranford High School, Cranford, NJ for the story about their high school English class and how they had students develop quizzes and study questions.

Also many thanks to Terri Bianco, TB Enterprises, for her support and terrific writing skills that turned my ideas into a book; Joe Hasenstab, President of Performance Learning Systems and my mentor, for writing the foreword; Barbara Brown of Phil Brown Fine Arts for editing and production management that made the book a reality; Kit Bailey of Second Look Proofreading and Editing for careful proofreading; Michael Brackney for his excellent index; and to Shari Resinger and Sylvia Filaccio, Victor Printing, for the layout, illustrations, and cover.

And last but not least, thanks to Barry Zvolenski, my right-hand man, for his constant and thorough support throughout the development of this book and all of my projects.

Foreword

More than 30 years ago, I received an outstanding recommendation for Steve Barkley to become a teacher trainer for us at Performance Learning Systems (PLS®). I knew in the first five minutes of the interview that Steve was going to be a superstar. It was the sparkle in his eyes, the way his voice danced with enthusiasm, and how he organized his thoughts about children and learning.

The next time I saw Steve was when we trained 60 teachers to be course instructors for the New York State United Teachers. Steve and I were two of six trainers teaching three groups of teachers. I was paired with Steve. I came in to do my shift and watched Steve work with the group. During a break, I asked around "How are things going?" The answer was enthusiastic: "Steve is great." So I said to Steve, "When we got here the group belonged to us and now they belong to you." Since then he has been the PLS spokesperson and missionary for sound teaching practices.

Since 1980 Steve has put endless effort into understanding learning and sharing his learning and passion with educators across the country and recently around the world. It's appropriate that effort be the focus of his third book because he exerts quality effort in all his undertakings.

I believe that the secret behind effort that leads to success in any field is "fire in the belly" which provides the perseverance to accomplish a vision. How else can we explain the high interest today in Internet blogs, computer chat rooms, video games, watching the NFL channel? People have passions and vision towards which they will exert effort.

Here's an example of effort I have exerted in my past 12 years. I play golf 150 days a year: As a golfer, I stand 120 yards from the hole. The wind is coming at me 15 to 20 miles per hour from left to right. I have to choose a club and a target. I pick my club and then I have to ask my mind that in this kind of wind and distance and location to the hole, how hard do I need to hit the ball to gain closeness to the pin? Do I trust that I can hit the ball at 120 yards (with a large and deep sand bunker in front of the hole and a steep embankment of green to the back)? Do I hit to a safe area or chance going at the hole? These steps involve deciding on something that counts. This is the most compelling part of golf: after-risk assessment, the "action." That is, telling the brain: "I am going to send the ball 120 yards. I need to target the left tree for a left to right drift, then land the ball in the broad area and get par. I do not risk a bunker and a steep pin placement on the green." Then I hit the ball and find out the consequences of my passion, vision, ability, and effort. That's me. Our students have passions too.

As educators, we have to face the challenges of how students learn differently today because of the amount of time they spend on computers and playing computer games. "Considering the amount of time spent on gaming, it is logical to assume that this gaming has affected the cognitive minds of teens today. William D. Winn, Director of the Learning Center at the University of Washington's Human Interface Technology Laboratory believes that this generation of children 'thinks differently than the rest of us. They develop hypertext minds. They can leap around. It's as though their cognitive structure were parallel not sequential" (Hostetter, 2000; Prensky, 2001).

"Patricia Greenfield made several discoveries of how this game generation's cognitive skills differ from previous generations. First, the game generation is more comfortable with visual-spatial skills, mental maps, and seeing the computer as a tool" (Greenfield, 1984).

Learning how to play video games is accomplished through "trial and error, observation, and hypothesis testing." (This is a good example of exerting effort.) Children develop cognitive skills vital in science: "inductive discovery." "Video games instruct children in decoding what symbols and graphics represent similar to learning what math or science symbols mean." They also develop multitasking skills "which require quicker responses as well as more concentration on the game" (Greenfield, 1984).

Effort is exerted in the classroom when there are successful skill and performance patterns defined (similar to those needed to be successful at golf), which are modeled, practiced, and coached. Effort to learn skill and performance patterns will be exerted by students if we create "compelling whys" for them—give them reasons for learning.

Learning the skill and performance patterns required in live events (real situations) that count (have consequences for the person) produce the greatest effort. Effort applied in these events is the result of one's passion.

Our job as educators is to create the habit of making effort occur within students. The future success of our society will be creating experts of our students. Research into experts, whether chess players or surgeons, shows producing an expert requires ten years of effort beyond the bounds of just "getting by" and expanding limitations by risk taking. As an example of such a risk, board certified doctors often refer their most difficult cases to other doctors who specialize in tough cases. They have successes. They also have deaths. The expert expands boundaries by taking risks. We need to develop experts.

K. Anders Ericcson, an editor of The Cambridge Handbook of Expertise and Expert Performance, "argues that what matters is not experience per se, but 'effortful study' which entails continually tackling challenges that lie just beyond ones competence" (Hostetter, 2006). Philip E. Ross in "The Expert Mind" concludes: "Motivation appears to be a more important factor than innate ability in the development of expertise" (*Scientific American*, August 2006). Personally, I believe that what separates good teachers from great teachers is continuing "effortful study" of the magical moves of best teaching practices. A person reading this book is doing "effortful study." So congratulate yourself.

For several years, I judged senior projects at the local high school-everything from rebuilding a 1960 Buick to working with the aged in a nursing home to tutoring math in 5th grade. I always asked the student one question: "How valuable was this project to your education?" The answer always was: "This is the most valuable thing I've done since I've been in school." As Steve's book argues, we need to motivate students to exert effort in compelling activities that count in the real world students will face.

If I returned to the classroom, I would "amp up" my effort to get students "amping up" their effort. Our students know our enthusiasm; they see and hear it. (Students in trouble often read our body language and intonation better than good students.) I would tend to organize cooperative learning groups and apply TV game show excitement on the most boring subject matter that must be learned. I would give more world applications to my subject matter. I would tell more fictional stories, imbedding my subject matter into a "compelling why" for learning it. I would ask students to invent their own "compelling whys." In short, I would "amp up" my effort to increase their effort.

Creating schools of the future will occur one reform at a time over perhaps generations. One day all classrooms will be exciting and useful with students exerting effort to learn. Steve's book on effort is part of that future.

Joseph K. Hasenstab

In the early 1970s, Joe Hasenstab founded Performance Learning Systems, Inc., a company dedicated to providing outstanding teacher training. Joe is an active proponent of positive change in education.

Introduction

A Fable

Once upon a time there was a small village settled at the foot of a towering mountain. Isolated from other villages, it consisted of many roughly made one-room huts, their roofs constructed of woven grass. A wide stream winding out of the mountain circled around the outskirts of the village. The villagers used this stream to get to next village; others had come to them by the same stream. They considered it their path. Their water source was from a well in the center of the village.

As we come upon them, we see people milling about, trying their best to live off the land. Some are preparing meals over open fires; others are fashioning poles. Some workers stab crude sticks into the hard ground in an attempt to soften it for planting. Many women are washing clothes at the well in the center of the village. The well has a small spout and a rustic pump with a handle that must be moved up and down rapidly to get a small stream of water.

Suddenly a fire breaks out in one of the houses, and the grass roof immediately leaps into flames. The villagers run to get their buckets and jugs and head toward the well in the village center. Men pump the well rapidly, and only a small stream of water comes forth. Still, the villagers fill their vessels in turn and run toward the flaming home.

None in the village thought to fill their jugs from the stream, which was adjacent to the house. In their minds, the stream did not consist of water; it was their path to the next village. They put their rafts on the stream; they did not drink from it or use it for putting out fires.

It's painful to picture such a scene—to see how people's perspective need only shift to gain success. If they could hear us, we would not be able to contain our desire to shout at them: "Use the stream! Use the stream!"

~~~

That's the way I often feel when I travel around the country and observe teachers in classrooms working so hard to get their students to make an effort to learn. Students are not making an effort and teachers are struggling to pull learning out of them or push them into trying harder. Teachers are stressed, pressured into accountability to prove adequate yearly progress. They seem to be prodding students, cajoling them—anything to meet the standards and realize the success they are mandated to achieve. So much time and energy are expended on "getting" students to work that teachers have lost sight of the beauty in creativity and in the spirit of learning that elicits genuine and natural effort. Students and teachers alike are working harder and enjoying it less. It's painful to watch, and it doesn't have to be that way.

Certainly there are classrooms where active, enthusiastic learning is taking place. To an outside observer, the difference between these schools and those where students and teachers are struggling— "working" at learning—stands out sharply. How, I wonder, can we change what is happening in these schools to resemble those where learning is an adventure or a challenge, where experiencing the simple task of exerting effort to achieve success actually feels good? It seems an old-fashioned value anymore, yet people who work hard do so because it feels good. Students can internalize that experience at a young age, and adopt a work ethic that can carry them through life.

Perhaps that "feel-good value" needs to be taught. Or perhaps value needs to be created by tapping effort in a way that feels good; tapping effort through motivation and because the learning involved becomes meaningful and fun.

In the book *The Game of School*, author Robert Fried makes a case that the whole process of schooling has taken on the aura of a game.[1] He goes so far as to claim that, "After enough time has gone by in which little or no authentic learning has taken place, teachers and students both adopt what I call the *false self of the pseudo-learner*" (or pseudo-teacher). He wonders why many students are saying school is so *borrriinnnggg* that no one listens. Or why all students have to do things the same way and "listen to the teachers" if they want to "be good."

Fried alludes to a situation where, due to pressures beyond their control, teachers are attempting to corral students into working hard rather than taking the time to create learning that will motivate students to want to make an effort. Instead, students discover it works best not to make waves, to exhibit "good" behaviors so they can get by unnoticed. Thinking about learning for learning's sake seems to have been replaced by the day-to-day task of just getting through lessons.

There is a danger in this situation. Getting by in school, making an effort only to take the test or "shining on" the teacher to pass by unnoticed creates repercussions in the workplace of today and tomorrow. Today's businesses and corporations are learning organizations. Information changes by the minute. Employee engagement is crucial in the private sector, as it directly impacts the bottom line.

The school culture of just getting by, studying to the test, and playing a game of learning translates to

---

[1] From *The Game of School: Why We All Play It, How It Hurts Kids, and What It Will Take to Change It* by Robert L. Fried, Copyright © 2005.

disengaged workers in the future. Disengaged people are disenfranchised, nonproductive, depressed, and not accountable. That sounds like too many high school students today.

How can we shift this perspective? How can we generate enthusiasm and motivation in students so they will want to exert effort without being prodded or, in some cases, actually bribed by their teachers? I think it entails a simple shift in our perspective and in our definitions of student effort, ability, task, and success. This shift in perspective can spell the difference between learning that is productive and enjoyable and learning that looks a lot like putting out a fire with small jugs of water pumped from a meager well.

This book focuses on ways educators and administrators can "use the stream" to tap into student effort, so that learning once again becomes creative, exciting, empowering, and engaging. Jump on your rafts and join me!

Chapter 1:
Formula for Success

High-speed gratification and TV spots highlighting only winning moments have sadly taken the concept of "effort" out of the driver's seat and into the blind spot. It's there, all right, but students don't seem to see it as a significant factor in achieving results.

Many students today believe it is ability that separates achievers from nonachievers. They see ability as fixed. One either has it or doesn't. They don't include in their thinking the piece about effort relating to ability and ultimately to success.

Effort remains secondary to ability. It's a means to an end. Students equate ability with success, relegating effort to the fuzzy world of "try." No one can "try" to do anything; they either do it or they don't. Try, for example, to turn the page of this book. No, don't actually turn it; "try" to turn it. See what I mean? Trying does nothing; *doing* does.

My goal would be to have students realize that exerting effort directly accomplishes something. Effort is the driver of ability. It usually entails carrying out something new or challenging, something we aren't necessarily comfortable doing. Applying effort slides us into a learning curve. We're learning as we make the effort. Once learned, it becomes easier as our ability increases.

Imagine parents sitting in bleachers by a field watching elementary students participating in a track meet. A fourth grader clad in gym shorts, Nike wanna be running shoes, and T-shirt prepares for the broad jump. He crouches, focuses, and off he goes! He leaps into the air when he hits the line, but apparently he did not have enough speed to reach the sand-filled pit, instead landing directly in a mud puddle. Trying not to laugh, the parents on the sidelines elbow each other and inevitably someone says, "Well, ya gotta give him an 'E' for effort! Yuk, yuk."

I'd like to suggest he gets an "A" for effort. In fact, he gets an A and a big "high five" *E* for effort. Why? Because it's the effort that counts. It's the effort that will increase his ability to be successful in future jumps. Not holding this perspective, however, the young man walks off the field despondent, embarrassed, and convinced he has no ability; he cannot succeed.

Where's the disconnect? The disconnect occurs because we often view increasing effort as directly increasing student success. We see effort as related to success rather than to ability. It's when students repeatedly apply effort that their ability increases incrementally, which over time improves performance leading to success. Expecting his or her efforts will quickly increase success may cause a student to quit when success is not realized.

Effort achieves results that, without that effort, would not occur. There is a consequence in not exerting effort. If the assignment is to write a sentence and the failure to do so results in the consequence of a bad grade, then taking out a page and beginning to write a sentence constitutes an effort. Completing multiplication tables from 2 through 4 is an effort. Picking up the oboe and playing scales is an effort.

Applying effort without some sort of ability leads nowhere—"trying" to perform brain surgery with no ability can be downright dangerous! Exerting effort adds tremendous value to ability. Ability increases from prior efforts, and additional effort further increases or improves ability. In fact, effort *multiplies* the chances for success in a task by increasing the ability to accomplish the task.

I view effort as a multiplier of ability, which then drives success. This happens even when initial ability is low. The only time it cannot work occurs when there is zero ability. Since this is rare, repeated effort almost always produces improvement. The effort expended results in increased ability—ability raised up, accelerated.

The next effort, then, even at the same level, allows for a multiplying effect as ability has increased from the previous effort, and now it is positioned to accelerate again, and on and on, exponentially. As ability is increased and subject to more effort, the spiral continues upward until success is achieved, seemingly effortlessly as it was the ability that tipped the scale to success. Ability was increased due to effort applied over and over again to an ability that kept improving. The last effort did not lead to success; it was the culmination of repeated applications of effort that increased ability.

The perspective we want here: *Focus on effort as increasing ability instead of effort being directly tied to success.* Tying effort directly to success can lead students to exert lots of effort that, while increasing ability, may not be immediately rewarded or acknowledged, and this can result in students giving up.

Many people today suffer from what I like to call "credit card thinking." Credit cards allow one to have the reward now and pay (exert effort) later. I often think I could lose weight if I could do it on credit! Losing weight is difficult for many people because it does take effort before we see the results. This is true for many successes in life. Instilling in students the connection between repeated effort and future success becomes an incredibly valuable skill students can rely on repeatedly throughout their lives.

Samuel L. Parker's book *212°—the extra degree* says: "At 211 degrees, water is hot. At 212 degrees, it boils. And with boiling water, comes steam. And with steam, you can power a train."

Effort can move water from simply hot to boiling because that one extra degree changes the *ability* of water to be steam, and that leads to success—powering a train.

The formula looks like this:

$$\underline{\text{EFFORT} \times \textit{Ability} + \text{Manageable Task}} = \textbf{SUCCESS!}$$

In Chapter 4, we will look at the "manageable task" aspect of the formula. For now, let's look at effort being tied to ability that ultimately leads to success. Effort is the heat; ability is the water; success is the steam.

Nature

Two schools of thought swirl around the attribute of ability. Both have some truth; each motivates differently. In the first, ability and intelligence are seen as relatively fixed. This assumes the student comes to class with his or her ability intact; it's natural, fixed at birth. It's a stable trait over which the learner has no control. Statements such as, "Students are either smart or not. There isn't much you can really do about it," or "Of course he's top notch; look at his gene pool," or "There is only so much I can do" come from the perspective that ability is fixed, or what is often referred to as Nature.

Nurture

The second school of thought contends intelligence and ability are changeable, evolving, nurtured by hard work and persistence. Those holding this view of ability believe students have control over how much their intelligence or ability can improve with work (effort), guidance, and focus. Educators holding the belief that ability can change, grow, and transition are less apt to give up on a student, preferring such statements as, "Kids are smart in so many different ways," or "He's going to get there. He just needs to see himself succeeding and rise to the occasion," and "Let's do this one step at a time, and I'm confident we'll get it done."

This Nature/Nurture phenomenon can affect a student's belief about him- or herself and how that belief translates into success. A student's belief often stems from how his or her parents or teachers view ability—fixed or changeable, Nature or Nurture. There is seldom open discussion about how a teacher or parent views a student's ability, but lingering doubts or feelings of pride are picked up by a student in everything a teacher or parent does or says or otherwise expresses.

The Pygmalion Effect

We have all heard stories of teachers who were fooled into thinking their classes were filled with gifted children and therefore treated them differently, only to find out that the students were randomly chosen, and not all gifted. Still, because of the teacher's perspective and belief about the students in the classroom, they were treated as if they had accelerated ability, and so they performed that way. This is known as The Pygmalion Effect.

A favorite example of this effect concerns a teacher who, on the first day of school, received a list with the names of her 30 students for the year. Next to each name was a number ranging from 127 to 157. Without being told, she assumed these numbers represented her students' IQ scores and felt honored to be teaching such an intelligent group. She worked hard all year to provide exciting and creative projects to keep these bright kids motivated. They responded well and were shining examples of good learners all year long.

When the school year was over, she made a point to thank the principal for giving her such an intelligent class and added how helpful it was to have the IQ scores on the first day. The principal looked confused, glanced at the roster she had with her, and said, "Those numbers aren't their IQs. Those are their locker assignments!"

That story exemplifies how our own belief system plays into our teaching and parenting. Certainly there is an innate intelligence and ability in each of us, and to the extent that it manifests in accomplishing tasks, we succeed on the strength of that ability. Yet the idea of a fixed ability with no room for improvement *other than SIMPLY topping prior performance* begs logic. Ironically it contradicts nature. In nature, everything changes and evolves. Why not ability?

Students operating with a fixed belief about ability— or who have teachers monitoring their performance and also harboring that belief—are only as good as their last performance. This is what they've got and that's it. There is no reason to exert effort or practice as that will probably not lead to measurable change. These students base their self worth on each task performed. Since they think they can't really improve their intelligence or ability, each performance is only a proving ground to beat the last performance. There's no expectation of improvement and thus there isn't much, if any. What you see is what you get. In contrast, those who believe their ability can change, improve, and evolve look at effort and persistence as the necessary fuel to drive success. They believe they have control over how much their intelligence or ability can improve. Failure serves as a signal—make a new plan, use a new strategy, and increase effort to achieve the success that they believe is achievable. To these learners, failure is not in falling down; it's in falling down and not getting back up—not learning from the fall so as to apply additional effort or make changes to redirect and achieve success.

Definitions

To underscore how the formula might work,

$$\frac{\text{EFFORT} \times \textit{Ability} + \text{Manageable Task}}{\text{BELIEF} \quad \text{VISION}} = \textbf{SUCCESS!}$$

let's look at the definitions associated with it.

Effort

Effort is the sweat that goes into a task. Time is required with effort. No time in, no success out. Basketball star Michael Jordan remained short for his age before growing tall in puberty and beyond. When he played basketball with the kids at his school, it's said he came home discouraged, telling his mom he was too small. His mother responded with something he never forgot. She said, "It's not the size of the boy in the game, it's the size of the game in the boy." No kidding!

The "size of the game" includes putting in time to become proficient in basketball. This requires persistence—keeping at it until the deed is done. Patience is needed as learning occurs. All effort benefits from practice, and practice requires repetition. Time, persistence, patience, practice, and repetition are important to succeed at the task, and they are equally important to keep us from being derailed. If we become impatient, we may give up or become negative. Impatience tests persistence; time may test the need for practice. Repetition may create impatience and boredom. Each ingredient in effort needs to be applied consistently and with balance.

Making effort is not an easy state to be in, you might say. And out of context, it probably isn't. But if effort is shown time and time again to multiply ability that leads to success, effort becomes a part of the larger formula. It is the driver, the fuel to completion.

When I was in high school, I wanted to play soccer. I wanted to be on the field when the game started. I specifically wanted to be the goalie. I tried out in my freshman year, got the uniform, felt "groovy" (that's what we said back then), and practiced with the team. And practiced with the team. And practiced with the team. And I sat on the bench every game during that first year.

In my sophomore year, I went back out for practice. I put in a lot of time. I was persistent. I did the moves over and over again. And I sat on the bench over and over again.

As a junior, I went out to practice and also sat on the bench every game *unless the team got far ahead or far behind.* Then I got to play! I got the experience of playing, of using the abilities I was honing in all that practice. Finally, my senior year, I got to play at the beginning of the game. I was the starting soccer goalie my senior year. Yes!

Others had started playing as freshman. They were more "natural" athletes. And I was able to play too. It just took the investment of time, persistence, patience, practice, and repetition. And the effort was worth it. (I still have the newspaper clipping high-lighting how we won the playoffs with MY help!)

By contrast, the one time I went skiing I put in a whole lot of effort getting up and down the slope. No success. No fun. I didn't give it any more effort, and I never learned to ski.

Ability

Ability is what we bring to the table. It consists of our skills, natural talents, and the areas of expertise in any situation. When we perform a task, we cannot change our ability at the moment of the performance. It is what it is. We can, however, improve our ability through effort on future tasks.

Our culture places higher emphasis on *ability* in school than other countries, such as Japan, which emphasizes *effort.* That ability dominates our thinking sets up a situation where students who have a lot of ability cease to work hard. Why bother? They can ace it anyway. Those who feel they have little or no ability also don't bother, but for different reasons—they "know" they will not succeed. Contrast that with the emphasis on the value of effort. The thinking here is that continued effort increases ability, so there is always room for success and improvement. No matter how much ability, effort increases it.

I have a natural ability to sing. I enjoy it. I'm good at it. So I joined our church choir only to discover that my travel schedule kept me from attending practice and rehearsal a good part of the year. Because I do have singing ability, however, I have been invited to stay in the group. This natural ability has served me well enough to continue to take part in the choir. In this context, ability "rules." One can only speculate, however, what might happen if I found the time to invest more effort (read: time, rehearsal, practice, etc.) in improving my ability to sing. Move over, Pavarotti!

Task

In the success formula, I refer to a "manageable task," and that has to do with the difficulty of the task. The perception that a task is difficult or easy tremendously influences a student's definition of success. If students believe they are tackling a task they consider "hard," they can easily erect an obstacle to success. "You can't expect me to do THAT! That's too hard!" Boom. Up comes the obstacle. Likewise, if students feel a task is too easy, they may feel they are able to do it without applying any effort.

Either one—the student who considers a task too difficult or one who considers it too easy—has given up ownership over his or her ability to succeed. It no longer has anything to do with ability; it's attributable solely to the difficulty of the task.

I recall in my freshman year of college receiving an A for my first college-level math class. You may be impressed until you consider the name of the course was "Fundamentals of Mathematics 101." After having taken calculus in high school my senior year, an A in the fundamentals of mathematics clearly reflected more on the degree of difficulty—in this case relatively easy—than on my effort or ability.

Little satisfaction occurs when a task creates an easy success. There is almost a feeling of dishonesty. It's also dissatisfying to throw one's hands up in defeat at an insurmountable task where no success is readily apparent. Tying success to the difficulty of the task equates with tying success to ability. If ability is fixed, then success occurs because of it. If the task is either too easy or too difficult, success occurs or does not occur in proportion to the difficulty of the task. Only in a belief in effort does ownership of the process occur.

Luck

Some people think luck has a role in student success or failure. "Lucky guy, aced the test" or "Just my luck. The test had *math* on it!" They think that success and failure are attributable to luck or chance. If learners are unsuccessful, they attribute failure to bad luck. If they succeed, they got lucky. Once again, there is no ownership and definitely no control by the learner.

A trophy in my home announces I won the Eight Ball Pool Tournament at a hotel where I stayed while traveling. I'm a pool hall champion—move over, Fats! The truth is I shot pool so badly that when it came time to shoot the eight ball, all of my other balls were still on the table and, by luck, all my opponents "scratched," making an error that cost them the game. As each person lost, I advanced further to become the champion.

I had similar luck on my first trip to the horse races. My winnings the first day had me thinking about quitting my day job. It only took one more trip to the track to realize the success had been based upon pure dumb luck (*dumb* being the operative word) and not upon any degree of difficulty, ability, or effort.

I Vote for Effort

Let's look at the formula again.

$$\underline{\text{EFFORT} \times \textit{Ability} + \text{Manageable Task}} = \textbf{SUCCESS!}$$

Rather than see effort as adding to ability—i.e., a little effort, a little success; a little more effort, a little more success; still more effort, still more success— I prefer to look at effort as a multiplier of ability, therefore having an accelerated impact on success.

One of my clients is a high school that has created small learning communities where students work with freshman advisors. Together we explored having all freshmen, both sexes, take a weight-lifting course as their physical education requirement.

In the weight lifting course, the instructor would benchmark students' current lifting ability and then lay out a workout plan whereby the student could track the increase in success as effort increased their ability. They could easily see how an increase in effort at each new level of ability multiplied their success in lifting weights.

That idea then segued into applying the same structure to a reading program in which increasing fluency could be recorded over a series of the students' practice sessions. The point was to underscore the value of effort in determining measurable success.

My contention is that, as effort is applied, ability grows and appreciates exponentially. Effort multiplies the ability when faced with a manageable task. Effort causes the ability to increase (appreciate) so that the same effort on the next trial produces greater results, because the effort is aimed at a higher level of ability. The payoff is higher.

Here's an all-American example.

Many people in this country have a lot of consumer debt. Statistically, the average amount of such debt is $8,000 per person. We have become a consumer society—so much so that, instead of referring to ourselves as American citizens as we once did, we are now called American consumers.

Jay Conrad Levinson and Loral Langemeier, advertising, marketing and financial gurus, jointly penned a book *Guerrilla Wealth: The Tactical Secrets of the Wealthy ... Finally Revealed.* One "secret" revealed was a system to eliminate consumer debt that makes my point about the multiplier effect of effort. Here's an outline of their plan.

> ***Step 1****: List all consumer debt—credit cards, loans, everything (don't be afraid). Include the following:*
> *1. Name of the creditor*
> *2. How much you owe*
> *3. Your minimum monthly payment*
> *4. Interest rate*
> *5. Factoring number.*

Step 2. Divide the total amount of the debt (item 2 above) by the minimum monthly payment (item 3) to get your factoring number. So, if you had $2,400 in total debt on one credit card and the minimum monthly payment was $120, your factoring number for that debt would be 20.

Step 3. Prioritize your list of debts by the factoring number, with the lowest factoring number at the top of the list and the highest factoring number at the end of the list. This is your "Priority Order of Payoff."

Step 4. Jumpstart your payoff plan by finding in your budget $200 that you can apply every month to your payoff plan. (Note: This may entail giving up a few things!)

Step 5. Using your "Priority Order of Payoff" list, apply the $200 to the first debt—the one with the lowest factoring number. This would be your lowest debt of the bunch. Example: If your payment on the $2,400 debt is $120, add $200 to it and make a payment of $320.[1]

Pay all the minimum payments required on the other debts, but continue the *effort* of adding $200 to your first debt. Once that debt is paid off, take what you were paying on that first debt (the $200 plus the minimum payment that you are now used to paying because your effort has increased your ability to pay more) and apply it to the next debt on the priority list. So now you have continued applying effort onto the next debt, accelerating the payment on that one until it disappears. Then on to the next, and so forth.

[1] From *Guerrilla Wealth: The Tactical Secrets of the Wealthy...Finally Revealed* by Jay Conrad Levinson and Loral Langemeier, Copyright © 2004 Live Out Loud. Reprinted with permission. All Rights Reserved. Visit www.liveoutloud.com.

Each time you increase your debt-paying effort, your ability to pay down a debt is successful. This requires a slight shift in thinking. You are tackling the task of debt reduction by applying consistent effort toward one task—the smallest debt—and when that has enabled you to reduce the debt, you redouble your efforts and apply more to the next debt, ultimately increasing your ability to pay and making your debt elimination plan successful.

Make cents??!

Increasing effort to multiply ability and achieve success serves as a mantra in the world of athletes. Athletes perform, and to perform well, they exert effort to increase their ability. Yes, some are natural athletes—some have more game in the man than others—but effort can level the playing field in sports as well as in student learning.

Educators, too, perform and can learn from athletes that a lot of effort early on leads to improvements in performance. Oftentimes teachers believe that attending a one-day workshop will do wonders for their performance. Instead, continued efforts toward improving one's teaching ability ultimately lead to success. It's a lifelong learning pattern. Effort improves performance. Ability improves. Additional effort shores up that improved ability, up and up, growing exponentially until success is the natural state, and effort is seen as the vehicle to get there. It's the heat, not the water.

In Chapter 2, we'll see what success looks like and how belief in that success stimulates a burning desire to increase effort. Imagine that!

Chapter 2:
Believing in Success

A deep and highly textured backdrop for all aspects of student learning lies in what students believe. Belief underlies effort in accomplishing a task. It shores up ability, and it's directly tied to success. Psychologists, philosophers, business leaders, athletes, religious leaders, and many visionaries have written volumes about the importance of belief or faith in achieving success. Joel Barker, Norman Vincent Peale, Earl Nightingale, Stephen Covey, Denis Waitley, Brian Tracy, Mark Victor Hansen, Zig Ziglar, Bob Proctor, and James Allen (author of the classic *As a Man Thinketh*) are but a few who come to mind as people who teach and live by the power of belief.

A book that motivated many people is Napoleon Hill's *Think and Grow Rich,* first published in 1937 and reprinted several times. Inspired by Andrew Carnegie, Hill spent a lifetime studying and documenting the lives and efforts of those who succeeded in gaining wealth by using what Carnegie called a "magic formula." The formula entailed incorporating beliefs in ways that ensured success. Hill studied people such as Presidents Roosevelt, Woodrow Wilson, and William Howard Taft; Thomas Edison, Charles M. Jennings Bryan, Clarence Darrow, and George Eastman of Eastman Kodak, to name a few, all of whom believed in working toward a goal with definite purpose.

It was Carnegie's hope that Hill would test and demonstrate the soundness of his success formula through the experience of men and women in every calling, and that the formula would be taught in all public schools and colleges so that others who may not realize how the rich do it could learn. Somehow I must have missed that class!

Kidding aside, why don't we spend more time focusing on students' beliefs? Certainly coaches pay tribute to the importance of belief in performance, and a number of teachers encourage students to believe in themselves. But we seldom set aside the time to actually *teach* students how their beliefs can better serve them as motivators. If our budding track star in Chapter 1 believed in himself, he would have pulled himself up from the mud puddle and walked proudly off the field, confident that his next attempt —or perhaps the one after that—would succeed.

Beliefs form and shape us. We live by them and seldom question them. Beliefs are formed by thoughts. We either create the thoughts ourselves or they are handed over to us, but every belief begins with a thought in the conscious mind. And the conscious mind can think anything it wants.

The subconscious mind is more robotic. It does what it's told by the conscious mind. A thought or idea comes into the conscious mind. Emotion is added to it, the thought becomes stronger, and it percolates to the subconscious mind. The subconscious mind then transmits the thought—now a belief—into the body, and the body acts. Praxis occurs—the integration of belief and behavior. Action is predetermined by thoughts and emotions coming together to form a belief. Results then reinforce the belief. (See Figure 2.1)

Thoughts are like air—we can't see them or hold them. Yet their power sets mankind apart from all other species. It's actually quite freeing. If you can control your thoughts, you control your actions, good or bad. When we think, we create an image, and that image controls how we feel. Feelings then cause action, and action creates results. It's an amazingly simple and incredibly complex aspect of being human.

Beliefs allow students to see the bigger picture. They are able to focus on the future, and their efforts to get to the future accelerate their ability to succeed. Researcher Benjamin D. Singer in "The Future Focused Role Image" claims "vision is the single most strongly correlated variable in high performing students and successful adults."

Figure 2.1

When There is Lack of Vision

Singer's studies of students concluded that low performing students had no vision of the future; their focus was short-term. They also held the Nature point of view that ability to shape their future was in the hands of fate and that they were powerless. High performing students had a much greater sense of control over their future, and thought in timeframes of five to ten years. They visualized increased ability and improvement, the Nurture point of view.

Low-performing or self-limiting learners cringe at the thought of failure because they believe their ability is fixed. They have accepted their limitations and have assumed that's the best they can be, not realizing that at any time they can simply choose different thoughts—thoughts that are not self-limiting. They may work to learn more, but their belief in their ability to learn is somehow diminished. They actually see what they consider poor ability as what keeps them from their success, never realizing that increased effort will increase ability. Some avoid any situation where learning may lead to failure; others who have met with little success in school frankly just accept failure as a way of life. They view themselves as incompetent and unable to succeed, and they believe effort will not produce success. This all stems from their beliefs, their thoughts.

In Cynthia's Kersey's book *Unstoppable: 45 Powerful Stories of Perseverance and Triumph from People Just Like You*, she tells the story of George Dantzig, an award-winning statistician and mathematician, when he was a student at the University of California at Berkeley. Dantzig often studied late into the night. One morning he overslept and arrived 20 minutes late for class. Seeing two math problems on the board, he quickly copied them down, assuming they were homework assignments.

It took Dantzig several days to complete the two problems, but he finally had a breakthrough and dropped the homework on the professor's desk. He was awakened at 8 o'clock Sunday morning by his professor, Jerzy Neyman, one of the founders of modern statistics. Neyman was beside himself with excitement. Dantzig had solved two "unsolvable" equations the professor had put on the board that day as mathematical mind-teasers. Even Einstein couldn't solve those problems. But Dantzig worked without any thoughts of limitation; he solved the problems because he did not have limiting thoughts; he did not know that he could not solve them.

Envisioning Success

High performing or mastery-oriented learners value achievement and see ability as improvable, not fixed. Failure, therefore, does not threaten the learner's sense of competence or self-worth; it serves as a tool to increase effort to shore up ability. These learners are responsible for what they learn because they know their success is a result of the effort they expend. They visualize their success and persist when struggling to learn. They know effort yields success, and failure is part of that success.

The subconscious mind responds to vision. It lives in the world of pictures and emotions. Students need to picture their success, to grasp the larger concept, as many athletes and performers do. Adding belief to vision provides the motivation needed to realize their vision, whether the vision is to become an astronaut or ace the next exam.

My own magic formula, therefore, is supported by belief and vision:

$$\frac{\text{EFFORT} \times \textit{Ability} + \text{Manageable Task}}{\text{BELIEF} \quad \text{VISION}} = \textbf{SUCCESS!}$$

How do we get students to picture their vision of success? The first stop? Goals. Setting goals allows students to envision achieving them. In *Motivating Students and Teachers in an Era of Standards,* Richard Sagor recommends that the "academic coach," as he calls educators, clearly outline the expectations that have been established for students and on which they will be assessed. He suggests including the state standards for the grade level, the district's standards, and the goals set for their learning by the teacher.[1]

Each goal has a rationale clearly explained, and then students are asked to commit to the goals. Once students understand the reason for the goals and the process of goal-setting, they are asked to affirm them publicly to the teacher and to the other students in the classroom, and then commit to their accomplishment over a specific time or until reaching a specified milestone. Then they set about designing action plans. Sagor recommends the process be student-centered and suggests students set out a "Goal Affirmation Sheet" listing what they want to accomplish and when they expect to achieve it. Parents or guardians sign the form along with the students. These accomplishments are specific, such as "reading 20 minutes each night."

Coaching Goal Setting

My recommendation would be to have students form their own "mastermind groups" teaming up to support each other's goals. Depending on the grade level, they could learn coaching skills to keep themselves focused and accountable. Collaboration on achieving the goals and holding celebrations when they were achieved would be encouraged.

Sagor's plan entailed following up the action plan phase with coaching by the teacher on how students might go about achieving their goals; reporting and reviewing results—a crucial step in looking at the goal—and checking results against it. Either approach, student teams or teacher coaching, helps make tangible the process of setting and achieving goals through action-planning or effort. A final crucial step: "Taking stock" to make sure the successes are celebrated will boost confidence and reinforce the vision and belief. Acknowledging the results fortifies the belief and creates the motivation to invest more effort.

I would recommend students develop their own personal goals aside from those the teacher outlines. While many will commit to those established by others, there is tremendous value in having students create their own personal goals, if for no other reason than to understand the value of the process.

Setting goals is a tried and true process. The steps are simple and powerful:

Set the goal: What does the person want to have, to do, or to be?

Visualize the goal. See it and feel it, in specific pictures.

Take action:

- Believe in the goal and the ability to reach it.
- Identify obstacles.
- Prepare for the future.
- Develop a plan and act on it.

Once those goals are affirmed publicly to other students, then students can begin to picture them, even draw pictures of themselves succeeding at whatever goal they have chosen. Here the teacher might talk about the importance of vision, cite biographies and other stories that show how someone's vision to succeed worked to their advantage. The classic children's book *The Little Engine That Could* by Watty Piper ought to be required reading from preschool through elementary. Alan McGinnis' *Power of Optimism* or Covey's *Seven Habits of Highly Successful People* and many other similar books might set a fire under many a middle school or high school teen.

Students could research the story and career of Bono, the Australian lead singer for the rock group U2 who at the end of 2005 was honored by *Time* magazine as "Person of the Year" along with Bill and Melinda Gates because of his vision for humanity. Teachers can share stories from their own career or upbringing. Stories evoke pictures, and pictures work to assist in envisioning the future. Students might better understand and commit to the curriculum goals educators shared with students when they can, in turn, connect them to their own personal goals.

"Visioning" Story

Steven Levy, a fourth-grade teacher at Bowman School in Lexington, MA created a powerful environment in which his fourth-grade students could envision a world they never knew. On the first day of class, he asked students to draw a picture of the ideal classroom. He prompted them with ideas and thoughts about what might be wonderful to have in the classroom. The homework assignment was to complete the drawing for the next class.

When students arrived in the classroom in September, however, they found nothing. No desks. No chairs. No books. All they had were the plans they brought with them from the homework assignment.

Uneasy students sat on the floor as Levy explained that, in order to better understand their social studies curriculum for the year—the life of a Pilgrim—and how they became a model for community, these students would use the fourth-grade classroom as their uncharted journey to a new land. They would learn how to create what they had envisioned as their ideal classroom—once they came to consensus and experienced a reality check about dimensions, scale, ratio, and the real feasibility of including a waterslide in the room. As they developed this primitive classroom together, they would build a community of fourth graders working, learning, and growing together, as the Pilgrims did years before.

Covering all aspects of the curriculum and more, Levy guided his students as they created tools, built their own desks, and raised money to obtain materials. Once they sold shares to businesses and individuals to buy materials, they selected and measured wood from the lumberyard. Since Pilgrims did not have nails, they used pegs instead. Thus they had to learn how to drill, to sand, and ultimately to stain, measuring the finished desks to understand dimensions, square feet, and area. Their involvement was huge, and at every obstacle, at each frustration, at every new turn, they harkened back to their vision of their ideal classroom created just as the Pilgrims they were studying would have done.

You can only imagine the effort, the increased ability, the motivation and the incredible sense of success and achievement they experienced when their desks and chairs were finally made and they could sit at them and get down to learning. As if they hadn't been doing that all along! At each step of the way, Levy videotaped interviews with students and their parents who shared the degree of effort students invested in the project. As they talked about their efforts, however, it didn't seem like effort at all. They shared the joy and enthusiasm they felt as they reached success after success in the process.

Another example of how goals create positive change can be found in Garden City High School, which underwent an academic makeover from 1993 to 2001 with the assistance of the High Schools That Work (HSTW) program sponsored by the Southern Regional Education Board in Atlanta, GA. One of the fastest growing communities in Kansas, Garden City is known for its feedlots and meatpacking houses. The goal for most students was simply to complete high school. GCHS student scores on the 1996 Kansas Assessment Tests put the school in the bottom 20 percent of all high schools in the state. The dropout rate in 1993-94 was 15 percent.

Clearly something had to be done. Under the wings of the coordinators for HSTW, Garden City began developing strategies—goals—for improvement in the high school and throughout the district. Some strategies included raising graduation requirements, requiring a senior project, focusing on literacy, and expanding the use of technology. There were strategies or goals within goals. The goal to raise graduation requirements included specifics, such as raising the total units from 20.5 to 26.5 and beefing up the science and math elements of the curriculum.

The success of this program was substantial, and what made it so was the inclusion of all students in the goals and strategies developed, tracked, and celebrated. A decided shift from the teacher-focused classroom to the student-centered classroom increased buy-in from students, and moving to a block schedule allowed teachers time for needed professional development.

In South Carolina, legislation was passed requiring schools begin developing career-inclusive individual education plans for 8th graders starting in 2006, with career planning starting for all students in grades six and seven. Focusing on the future, using school to create the image of future careers creates the motivation to connect current requirements to their ultimate bottom line in business or technology. This in and of itself generates the desire for more effort. Do students have to follow the career they select in school? Of course not. Some will and some won't. But they experience the process of focusing on a future endeavor and applying current effort to achieve it.

While writing my book, *Quality Teaching in a Culture of Coaching*, I came across many successful models used by personal and professional coaches. Figure 2.2 depicts one appropriate for student effort.

Point A is Where We Are; Point B is Where We Want To Be. At Point A, we already have a hidden obstacle—fear, insecurity, or a belief we can't achieve beyond a certain point. This obstacle pops up as we are moving from Point A to Point B. Sometimes the obstacle represents a real limitation, such as a lack of schooling or need for more practice or desired coaching. Those limitations can be remedied by action, yet an internal obstacle may still exist.

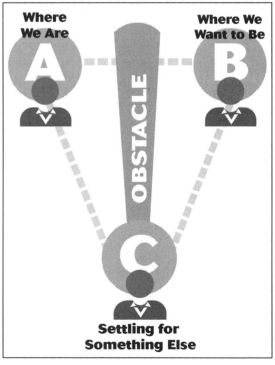

Figure 2.2

If we stop at that obstacle without going through it—if our picture of success (Point B) is not strong enough or compelling enough, then we drop down to Point C: Settling for Something Else.

In the triangle created from Point A to the obstacle to Point C reside negative beliefs, guilt, limiting thoughts and behaviors.

When we are committed to our goal and *believe* we can achieve it—visualize its achievement— then our thoughts and behaviors and actions can move through the obstacle. (See Figure 2.3.) In the triangle on the right side of the diagram, from

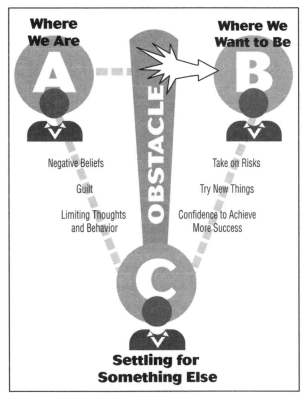

Figure 2.3

Point B to the obstacle to Point C, there lies the opportunity to take on more risk, to try new things, to achieve more with the confidence that our efforts and our abilities create success. We believe it, and it happens. The left triangle focuses on looking backward, limiting thoughts; the right triangle represents looking forward, self-achieving behavior, belief in success.

This model aptly depicts the difference between those with low-performing behavior, with limiting thoughts and beliefs telling them that nothing can be done, and those with a high-performing, mastery-oriented focus on success. Effort is a multiplier of ability when applied to a manageable task, and that leads to success, as long as there is an accompanying belief that success is achievable. Expending effort over and over without belief or faith in an image of success, however, is like blowing up a balloon that has been ripped apart and sewn back together. It's a lot of hot air, a lot of effort, but no one really believes the balloon will ever become filled.

Envisioning the future, the goal, underscores an essential human need to continue on. In 1950, Florence Chadwick set a world record when she swam across the English Channel from France. The following year, she swam the opposite way, from England to France, making history as the first woman to swim the channel from both shores.

In 1952, however, Chadwick experienced failure. She accepted the challenge of swimming 26 miles from Catalina Island to Palos Verdes, CA. The waters were cold and sharks were present, but that did not result in failure to reach the shore. After 15 hours of rough swimming, she could no longer see any sign of the coastline because a heavy fog shrouded the area. With her goal out of sight, Chadwick lost the will to continue and essentially went to Point C in our example above: she settled for the escort boat.

When asked why she stopped, Chadwick said, "It was the fog. If I could have seen land, I could have finished. But when you can't see your goal, you lose all sense of progress and you begin to give up."

A poem that can summarize the value of dreams, beliefs, and faith in one's ability was written by Debbe Kennedy and precedes Joel Barker's training program, "The Power of Vision."

Our Dreams in Action

Dreams give us hope.
Hope ignites passion.
Passion leads us to envision success.
Visions of success open our minds to recognize opportunity.
Recognition of opportunities inspires far-reaching possibilities.
Far-reaching possibilities help us enlist support from others.
Support from others keeps us focused and committed.
Focus and commitment foster action.
Action results in progress.
Progress leads to achievement.
Achievement inspires dreams.

Dreams give us hope.[2]

And that's worth thinking about.

Chapter 3:
Appreciating Success

The Gallup Organization's Strengths Revolution

Alachua County Schools in Gainesville, FL underwent a study conducted in the 1980s by SRI Perceiver Academies, Inc., an arm of The Gallup Organization. Unlike most studies, aimed at discovering what plagues low achievers or at-risk students, this study was aimed at *high*-achieving students from fourth to eighth grade to determine what influences these successful students had from parents, counselors, guardians, or other significant adults that translated into high-achieving values.

They discovered that adults in these students' lives showed a constant and positive focus on each student's future—where they were going, what it looked like when they got there. Parents provided direction; coaches talked of expectations and modeled successful behaviors; counselors worked with them to create visions of a successful future.

The children felt they had advocates standing behind them, providing emotional support, recognition, celebration, and concentrated time with parents or other adults. In every case a picture of the future—an image with an associated positive emotion—contributed to their success. These pictures of future success then motivated current effort.

Future pacing—looking at a picture of the future—constituted the payoff for the students' investment in effort and ability. This study underscores that creating a goal and a picture with the student spells the difference between a student who succeeds and one who settles for his or her perceived limitations.

The Alachua study paralleled another conducted by The Gallup Organization over the past 30 years, which surveyed more than 1.7 million employees in 101 companies from 63 countries to learn where, when, and how focus was placed on employees' strengths, natural talents, and high performance, and what resulted. Among the many questions, one specifically asked: "At work, do you have the opportunity to do what you do best every day?"

Globally, only an alarming 20 percent of employees in the organizations surveyed felt their strengths were in play every day. Instead, most were working to overcome perceived shortcomings at their job. In most organizations, in schools, and in society itself, our focus continues to be on weaknesses, what is missing, what needs to "get better."

In *Now, Discover Your Strengths*, Marcus Buckingham and Donald O. Clifton, Ph.D., also of The Gallup Organization, contend most organizations—and that would include schools—concentrate on what they call two flawed assumptions: [1]

1. *Each person can learn to be competent in almost anything.*
2. *Each person's greatest room for growth is in his or her areas of greatest weakness.*

As we focus on weaknesses in our society, we find them. What we think about, we get. We look for gaps in skills, find them, and then focus on damage control, trying to "fix" (remediate) an employee or a student who doesn't seem to comply with the rules of the day. In their survey, Gallup discovered that the world's most successful managers seem guided by two very different assumptions:

1. *Each person's talents are enduring and unique.*
2. *Each person's greatest room for growth is in the area of his or her greatest strength.*

I would like to think educators believe in those assumptions; that that's what keeps them—and me—going. Yet educators are constantly faced with placing student successes—their strengths, their efforts, and their abilities—into a box of structures and standards of achievement that are static even though students, being human, are not. Rather, students resonate with talents and successes and visions and feelings that guide their future and their

---

[1] From *Now, Discover Your Strengths* by Marcus Buckingham and, Donald O. Clifton, Copyright © 2001 The Gallup Organization. Reprinted with permission. All Rights Reserved.

achievements and, as educators, our role is to guide them toward success. Given that we need to live within a certain prescribed structure to measure student success—as well as our own successes and achievements—I am nonetheless intrigued and inspired by the possibility of a focus on strengths and positive future pacing that can attain both the success and the "mandated achievement" we strive for. This can occur while also fulfilling the time-honored practice of developing children into high-performing, productive adults complete with the qualities of leadership, integrity, and a confidence in knowing that their efforts, whether they have the specific talent for the task or not, will nontheless pay off. Shouldn't we help students, as whole persons, to understand what they do best so that when they are eventually employed, they will create opportunities to develop those strengths?

Concentrating on Strengths and Future Success

Looking at what we do well, at strengths instead of weaknesses and at future success instead of past failures, can shift the role effort plays. While pure effort can result in successfully completing a task, unless the natural strengths of an individual aren't tapped and built upon, burnout can result before any improvement becomes apparent. Persistence lies at the core of improvement in performance, yet it also requires some other kind of fuel to foster a continuation of the learning process.

Focusing on strengths not only provides the fuel,

but also serves as a reminder and a tool to use in situations where talent or strength may be lacking—where the "flesh is willing but the spirit is weak." This focusing of student's strengths can deepen his or her experience of success. Remembering the feeling of success with Task A charges up the student to complete Task B, one that may not utilize the student's particular talents. This does not mean that the student is not capable of tackling Task B or that he or she cannot attain it. Rather, the student acknowledges that he or she has a talent for A, and that for B there is simply a "nontalent," not necessarily defined as a weakness.

Looking at lower performance for Task B as non-talent defuses the sense that it has to be worked at with great effort and possible angst. Rather, the student can, where possible, apply the same strengths he or she uses to succeed in Task A to Task B.

Successful people are constantly employing their strengths to overcome or override what may be considered "nontalent," abilities that just don't seem to take off as others do.

Buckingham and Clifton define strength as "consistent near perfect performance in an activity." They cite such greats as investor Warren Buffet, golf pro Tiger Woods, and songwriter Cole Porter as having strengths, to be sure, but who, rather than downplaying where they were *not* superstars, leveraged where they were strong and built on those for their success. Buffet's strength is patience, not taking entrepreneurial risks. Woods is a great driver and putter—and can't get out of sand traps. Cole Porter was a terrific songwriter but did not fare well in scripting characters in plays.

Obviously these "weaknesses" did not deter these successful men. Instead they focused on what they did well. What they focused on, they got. It's true for everyone. They discovered their strengths and built their lives around them. Right behind these greats (well, not *too* far behind!) sits yours truly. I learned in high school that I had the ability to connect with people, to speak candidly and with humor before an audience. I had no fear of public speaking. I enjoyed it. My career as an educator and a trainer has been built around that capability, those strengths.

As I built my career, I became aware I needed to gain the recognition and credibility my profession demands by publishing books and articles—I needed to write. I began putting my thoughts about education to paper, wrestling with rewrites and addenda. Finally I was finished and handed my manuscript to a trusted colleague.

"This is plain awful," said my friend bluntly, a strength I admire in him. "It's boring. It's repetitive. It's good information, but it's not you." He suggested that rather than write, I rely on my strengths as a speaker and speak to my reading audience using a Dictaphone or similar device.

I gave it a try and, as a result, this book and others like it, along with many published articles, are products of that good advice. I work with my assistant who transcribes my spoken thoughts, and my Contributing Editor Terri Bianco who has the knack—the strength—of being able to take my ramblings, thoughts, and insights and make good sense of them through the written word. Rather than struggling to learn how to write, attend writing classes, or spend hours laboring through edits, I operate from my strengths, and Terri can do the same. It's a win-win, and no one feels "weak" or inadequate.

Global activist and author Lynne Twist served as Executive Director of The Hunger Project, a strategic organization partnering with 13 developing countries to provide strategies that empower people to achieve lasting progress—teaching them how to fish, rather than providing the fish itself. Author of *The Soul of Money*, Twist has worked around the world with people as diverse as Mother Theresa and Bill Gates. She has witnessed a lot of suffering and possesses tremendous compassion.

As a result, whenever she speaks about her work, she inevitably cries. Faced with the prospect of speaking before the United Nations, Twist panicked, wondering what she would do if she started crying. Typically, she would stop speaking for an embarrassing few moments until the emotion passed.

Her coach, however, gave her some guidance that helped her focus on her strengths—her conviction, empathy, understanding, and passion for what she believed in. He suggested she focus on her intention, focus on the compassion she held as she spoke, and talk right through the tears. She subsequently succeeded at the United Nations, and is successful now when she speaks to organizations about her Soul of Money Institute. After her introduction, she acknowledges the audience, lets them know generally what she will be talking about, and then says, "And I will probably cry. I always do." It has become her trademark. And it has not diminished her power of conviction.

A realtor in my town is unusually tall—about 6'7". His ad in the local newspaper every week is long and slender with a full body photo of the man and the heading, "John North. A Head Above the Crowd." Salesmen are notorious for using their strengths to their advantage.

And finally, we only need to look to learning styles to realize that our preferences are our strengths. A visual learner who recognizes he or she is visual can use that ability to advantage. The visual person will be the one taking notes during a group discussion or meeting and will have the information long after everyone else has forgotten it. People who organize information globally, seeing the big picture and making intuitive leaps, but aren't so hot at the details in-between, are smart to surround themselves with others who tend toward the sequential step-by-step approach. Failing that, there is a whole industry of organizers and other devices designed to focus the global learner.

It's been said that James Earl Jones, a great narrator with a beautiful deep voice, stuttered as a child. Yet he loved the written word, he loved poetry. As the story goes, an astute teacher saw in Jones his strengths in appreciating language, and he allowed the boy to recite one of his poems in class. Relishing the words he had painstakingly put to paper, Jones recited his poem with nary a stutter. One teacher who focused on what works, what's right, and what's powerful ultimately elicited more of the same.

To recognize strengths or talents in students, Buckingham and Clifton suggest noticing what they call "yearnings," a desire that often forms in early years to be or do something that remains rather consistent throughout school. James Earl Jones apparently had a yearning for language, initially stemming from his admiration for the uncle who recited *Julius Caesar* to the farm fields. Another indication of students' strengths reveals itself when students tend to learn something rapidly when it falls along the lines of their talents; it seems to come naturally and they learn it quickly and well. Finally, an expression of satisfaction presents itself on the faces of students who achieve something within their specific realm of talents or strengths.

For an example of such a talent, let's look at one of 34 themes The Gallup Organization has identified and described in *Now, Discover Your Strengths*. This theme is called the "Developer," one that most likely applies to many educators. The Developer theme identifies individuals who see the potential in others. They seek to create experiences and activities that will help others grow, show improvement. When they see someone else improving, they are fueled to keep going themselves; their level of satisfaction goes up as they help others.

Suppose a student is asked to write a summary of a chapter in an English class. The task is a manageable one: He or she knows the material well, yet is stymied by a hesitancy to use creative writing skills; he or she is blocked. Since one of the student's strengths or talents lies in the Developer theme, he or she might be a good candidate to serve as a mentor to someone else given a similar assignment. The first student's desire to help the other provides the impetus to follow suit and create his own summary.

My point in all this lies in noticing not only the level of a student's efforts toward a task, but to combine the belief in success—the vision of the future success—with something that is already a driving force for each student's individual talents or strengths.

Closer to home, we can look to Howard Gardner's multiple intelligences, captured in the Performance Learning Systems, Inc. graduate course, *Purposeful Learning Through Multiple Intelligences*®. Noticing the child's tendency toward one of the now eight intelligences identified by Gardner, educators can amplify student effort by utilizing the strength, talent, or intelligence already at the student's disposal.

To illustrate, let's look at the story of Bradley as submitted by educator Sarah Lovelidge of North Bend Elementary in Harford County, Maryland.

Bradley's Breakthrough

It was a push-comes-to-shove time of the school year when teachers were scrambling to make sure that kids had the right skills to make it through and succeed on the big test. The guest teacher, a specialist, had been invited into the third-grade classroom with a tried-and-true lesson on reading to perform a task. The classroom teacher was able to sit back and watch her children work, giving her an opportunity to observe interactions and skills.

The guest teacher started by explaining the task at hand and walking through an example. The children were to read a set of instructions that included diagrams, much like the directions one would use when putting together a toy that came in parts. The kids were quiet and attentive with the unfamiliar guest teacher, a little bit apprehensive as they approached this very different type of task. The directions were to create the Delta Dart, a specially designed paper airplane. Supplies were distributed along with the page of instructions.

Quiet descended on the room as the children began their task. Little fingers worked on the paper as the children read each section and tried their best to apply the instructions and the diagrams to the uncooperative paper. Folds appeared unbidden. Edges crumpled. Frustration came quickly to several students. They were the "high flyers," the ones to whom everything came easily. These were kids who had been reading since kindergarten, whose parents had exposed them to every experience possible. They were used to success. Here was a task that did not come easily to many of them, and they were not accustomed to that.

One of the other students was Bradley. Bradley was a quiet child, one who worked hard but had yet to conquer the intricacies of reading. He was a resource student who left the room for a few hours each day for intensive instruction tailored to his special needs. This alone set him apart from the other students. The teacher knew that Bradley had a good solid upbringing with a family who cared deeply about his success in school. Behavior was never a problem, only the disability in reading. This made Bradley one of the lesser lights in the classroom. He was a second-class student and already knew that by third grade.

As the minutes ticked on and children struggled to get their planes folded, suddenly Bradley jumped up. His face was alight with the joy that comes from success. He had followed the detailed diagrams and created a beautiful paper plane, exactly like the instruction sheet showed. By this time, a few of the more able readers, unused to failure, had begun to cry. Here was a task that was closed to them, and they were not used to that. Bradley moved around the classroom with the blessing of the guest and classroom teachers, giving a hint here, helping with a fold there. The other students gratefully accepted his help, coming as it did from an unusual quarter.

He had been able to use his exceptional ability in visual-spatial intelligence, a skill that he had come by naturally and honed with years of experience at his dad's side in the family garage. Forget reading for the moment; Bradley had followed the diagrams to success. He was easily able to visualize what the tiny arrows and dashed lines meant. One step at a time, he had created his masterpiece.

It was a defining moment in Bradley's school career. Even though this was just one rung of his ladder to success, he was now a verified star of the classroom. He had shown himself to be very capable in his own special intelligence, which somehow more than made up for a lack of natural ability in the more traditional verbal-linguistic intelligence. Bradley went on to have a successful year in third grade. Having had the success of creating the Delta Dart, and the crowning glory of offering aid to the best students, he was now an equal in the classroom. His effort increased, with consequent gains in all areas of the classroom.

Though the teacher lost touch with Bradley as the years went by, the story stayed with her. Bradley's success and increase in effort, his finding a place in the classroom had come from the one moment when his special intelligence was found and stamped with approval by his peers and teacher. The lesson to the teacher was that finding each child's intelligence strength was a hugely important key to evoking greater effort in all areas.

Appreciative Inquiry

The idea of emphasizing strengths has inspired a rapidly advancing approach to organizational development called Appreciative Inquiry. Developed by David Cooperrider of Case Western Reserve University, Appreciative Inquiry represents a departure from traditional change management in its focus on what works rather than on problems, issues, or what is *not* working. Simplistically, it's the glass-half-full approach over the glass-half-empty, and its ramifications for framing organizations are huge.

Cooperrider's wife, an artist, introduced him to the concept of an "appreciative eye." In every piece of art there is beauty. In the Appreciative Inquiry or AI approach, as it is called, "appreciative" also refers to growing in size or significance, such as an investment appreciating in value, or a trickle of water that appreciates into a stream (one that could douse the fires described in our Introduction fantasy!). "Inquiry" refers to the beginning of the AI process where questions are posed to elicit positive rather than problem-based responses.

Imagine, for example, if instead of being asked in a

faculty meeting why test scores were down, teachers were asked, "What kinds of things do you do to keep your children's interests high in what might be considered a dry subject?" "How is it that you can build trusting relationships with so many of your students?" "What do you do to balance fun and discipline in the classroom?" Imagine the excitement as teachers shared their beautiful and creative successes rather than their anguished attempts to solve problems. A focus upon the details of success—as opposed to a focus on what's *not* working—produces increased motivation and effort on the part of the teacher.

The inquiry portion of the AI process becomes the springboard for discussion, discovery, and delivery of options based not on what is wrong, but on what is right, what works well, where the strengths lie.

A primer on Appreciative Inquiry can be found in the national bestseller, *The Thin Book of Appreciative Inquiry* by Sue Annis Hammond. Hammond distills the theoretical concepts of Cooperrider's theory, which can be equally utilized in a one-on-one session, class-room event, or complete systems reorganization. Often, the AI approach can be implemented with minimal exposure but a definite mind-set shift in perspective.

The basics include inquiring—discovering—what is working, what feels good, what we are doing when it *does* feel good, and how to repeat this positive, working pattern in the next event/task/opportunity. That defines the beginning of the AI process, followed by discovery and action planning based on the themes defined in the initial inquiry.

A PLS process I often use called "Questions for Life®" focuses on questions that have cue words to elicit a certain type of thinking among students: "summarize" or "analyze"; "what if?" or "what insights?" are cues to elicit thinking patterns that tell the receiver how to respond. In AI, the questions—inquiries—are always phrased in terms of what positive emotions, events, circumstances, and successes one recalls.

A more in-depth AI process, described in *Appreciative Inquiry: Change at the Speed of Imagination* by Jane Magruder Watkins and Bernard J. Mohr, identifies and prescribes five specific steps to get a group, an individual, or an entire organization to a place of identifying and then acting on their strengths, each of which requires a certain amount of effort and ability, but each, again, shored up by a positive, future-paced focus rather than an attitude of "getting better."

Without dissecting an involved and also evolved process of managing and creating change in organizations, suffice it to say that a focus on the strengths and positive motivators of people, including "student-people," provides an intriguing and powerful model for education. Its accord with my own formula of "exhibiting effort that becomes a multiplier of ability when applied to a manageable task"

$$\frac{\text{EFFORT} \times \textit{Ability} + \text{Manageable Task}}{\text{BELIEF} \quad \text{VISION}} = \textbf{SUCCESS!}$$

becomes fortified by the added ingredient of a belief in success coupled with a focus on one's strengths:

what's working, what's positive, what will make you go above and beyond?

In a TV commercial for Budweiser beer, airing during a Super Bowl, a Clydesdale colt is sniffing around the barn where the famed Budweiser wagon is stored. The colt approaches the harness and puts his head into it as the viewer notes the colt has a long way to go to fill that harness. Still, the young horse moves into it, leans against it, and makes an effort to pull the wagon usually pulled by 12 two-ton Clydesdales.

He makes the effort, but it doesn't move. Then the colt makes another effort, pulling and leaning into the harness, and now we see the young horse slowly hauling the wagon out of the barn and into the clearing outside. Only then do we see the heads of two full-grown Clydesdales quietly pushing against the back of the wagon, unseen by the young colt, but there nonetheless to allow him to experience the completion of the task in a successful fashion.

These two large Clydesdales represent to me belief and a focus on one's strengths—two quiet but powerful drivers to aid in the legitimate and genuine act of exhibiting real effort.

Next, let's see how to capitalize on these dynamic forces by applying them to efforts that begin somewhat small or perhaps more attuned to talents—tasks that are manageable and therefore achievable. These encourage persistence toward successful attainment of results—not only for the student, but also for the teacher, the administrator, the school, and the parents. Success is bright and positive and filled with the joy of learning. Anything we can do to support "efforts" that lead to success becomes fair game.

Chapter 4:
Managing Success

A combination of belief in one's ability, envisioning success, and focusing on the end result has accomplished miracles throughout the ages. We all know stories ranging from the lives of athletes to events in yesterday's classroom where individuals never lost sight of their vision and ultimately succeeded. "Ultimately" is the operative word, as success often comprises components that build and build until the vision and the success manifest, sooner or later, depending on the difficulty of the task.

Success starts with a vision or belief. That is followed by effort, ability, and tasks that are achievable, one at a time. The importance of a vision or belief is again underscored here, because initial effort frequently receives no visible sign of a payoff. There are key elements within the exertion of effort that create a motivating force, much as moving water from 211 degrees to 212 degrees changes it from hot water to boiling water and ultimately to steam, as pointed out by Samuel Parker in his book *212°—the extra degree.*

Requirements of Effort

Time

Effort requires time. Without putting in time, effort goes missing. And the time must be quality. "It isn't the time you put in, but what you put into the time that really counts," according to an anonymous source.

Persistence

Effort also relies on persistence. Persistence requires a definite purpose backed by a burning desire for its fulfillment. With persistence, there is a plan in place, expressed in continuous action, and a refusal to entertain discouraging thoughts or suggestions designed to shatter the belief or vision, even if we ourselves are creating the negative obstacles. With persistence comes a need for patience as the plan unfolds and achievements are discovered.

Practice

Effort requires practice. It means consistently doing

what needs to be done until it is executed correctly. This is not a "click-and-go" event. It requires guided practice followed by more individual practice.

In our credit card society, consumers buy on credit and then make the effort to pay for it, as mentioned earlier. I often wish I could lose weight that way. Click on "25 pounds" in the doctor's office; walk out with an immediate weight loss that would then motivate me the next morning to start exercising to keep it off. Educators, however, have to instill the notion of applying effort and practice that leads ultimately to success. This is why the picture of the future is so important. While every play in football is designed to be a touchdown (the vision) each play may entail inching the ball down the field toward the goal.

Repetition of Success

Finally, effort requires repetition of success so that it becomes ingrained, internalized, and automatic. Driving a car, getting dressed in the morning, playing a piano piece, or completing multiplication tables are achieved through time, persistence and patience, practice, and finally repetition of what worked. What works then becomes a success that motivates future effort toward the envisioned goal.

Manageable Tasks

Oftentimes the perceived manageability of a task determines how learners feel about their success or failure. A task may be perceived by learners as "hard" or "easy." If it's deemed too hard, learners approach the task thinking (believing) they can't be successful. If the task seems too easy, learners cannot justify taking much credit for their efforts. Instead they attribute their success to their innate or learned ability, forgetting that even given their talent in a particular task, effort is required and should be acknowledged.

Whether hard or easy, attributing success or failure to the difficulty of the task takes the ownership of that success or failure away from the learner and his or her efforts. Excuses or rationalizations are made about the task based on its being too hard (therefore he or she failed), or a "piece of cake," not requiring any effort at all.

Likewise, students who attribute their success or failure to chance or luck also give away their ownership and responsibility for their efforts. Luck or chance, not their efforts, becomes the reason for their achievements. When students assign their success or failure to the difficulty of the task or luck, it creates an obstacle to their understanding of the role effort and ability play in achieving their vision of success.

Good teachers understand the need to provide students with tasks that are manageable. Tasks that are manageable and can be achieved through effort—effort that requires time, persistence, practice, and ultimately becomes automatic—result in accomplishments that can then be celebrated and reinforced. Does this mean dumbing down tasks to the lowest denominator so even the smallest effort is deemed successful? Not at all. It means taking a vision of success, a goal, and breaking it down to manageable parts so it can be accomplished. It often means working backwards from the goal to identify the choices students need to make to achieve that goal. Without that kind of blueprint, some tasks simply aren't achievable, no matter how great the effort nor how strongly desired the vision.

Yet there is a caution here. Differentiating instruction so as to make it manageable can be overdone. The tasks can be overmanaged to the point where a student's future is at stake. In *Updraft Downdraft: Secondary Schools in the Crosswinds of Reform*, authors Marilyn Crawford and Eleanor Dougherty identify a prevailing trend in secondary education that channels one group of students toward postsecondary education (dubbed "Updraft" students) and others who are left to receive their secondary degree only or to simply drop out, called "Downdraft" students.[1] This downdraft group falls into an older system of tracking students according to credits and grades, planting them onto a bell curve, and sorting out success and failure based on ability to earn a diploma, albeit one that does not necessarily guarantee future success or job attainment. The authors refer to the system as "social reproduction."

Figure 4.1 illustrates the forces that cause teachers and schools alike to "differentiate" the opportunities for those clearly headed toward higher education and those whose bottom line goal is that weak diploma. Teachers focus on keeping order in the classroom over achievement. Some negotiate with students to behave in exchange for what the authors term "school knowledge"—knowledge that has its place and meaning in school but nowhere else.

[1] From *Updraft, Downdraft: Secondary Schools in the Crosswinds of Reform* by Marilyn Crawford and Eleanor Dougherty. Reprinted with permission. Copyright © 2003 Rowman and Littlefield Publishing. All Rights Reserved.

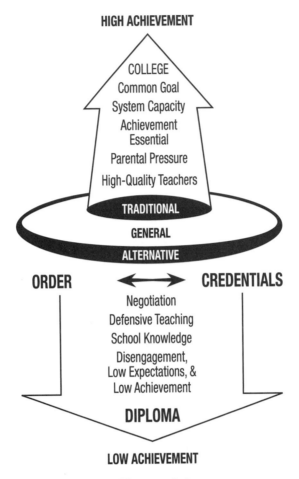

Figure 4.1

Teaching can become "defensive" as they control the knowledge, the classroom environment—anything to keep students passing and moving on at the expense of meaningful learning or achievement.

The "updraft" students, however, are expected to succeed. There is a common belief among teachers, parents, and the students themselves that higher education is a must. Good teachers gravitate to those students, the system readily accommodates them, and options to study and learn independently are a given. This is as it should be, since it is assumed they will undoubtedly enjoy that type of flexibility and autonomy as an employer or employee in a higher-level position in the future.

Updraft students see a direct connection between the schoolwork they are doing and their vision of success in the outside world. Downdraft students are not given that connection—the vision—or time has not been spent reinforcing it. Effort, of course, suffers tremendously as the downdraft students see no point or purpose in it.

Missing from that Pygmalion scenario in my mind is any emphasis on the value of learning, whether manageable or challenging, differentiated or based on fixed standards. It's as if students who are focused solely on a high school diploma, which in their minds terminates their education, were admonished: "Eat your dinner or you can't have any dessert." Just as they would shovel the meal into their mouths to get their reward, they likewise take the course credits required, get the grades, go through the motions, and end up with dessert. Empty calories, in many cases.

Students who value learning, however, eat it up. Just as they eat their meal knowing its nutritional value, knowing the food is delicious, that it feeds the body and mind, that it is good for them *and* that they also get to enjoy dessert, so, too do they also devour learning with anticipation and the foreknowledge that it is good for them. They look for opportunities to learn, to create, and to extend beyond the course material; to study independently and actually have fun learning.

The importance of being a lifelong learner is often assumed and not taught: Belief in it typically separates achievers from those just getting by. Updraft students somehow learn about the value of learning, how to be lifelong learners. Downdraft students may need to be taught.

Not a bad addition to a school curriculum, "Lifelong Learning 101." Once one appreciates learning for learning's sake, understands the value in it now and into the future, he or she can see it for what it is. Students understanding what learning itself is about will know their limitations and their strengths in tackling a task or assignment. They will know when to dive in at all costs even when the task seems daunting, or when to do what's required to meet the assignment, saving their learning muscle for tasks that better serve their goals and visions. Being a lifelong learner naturally leads to differentiating between tasks that are manageable and those that may not be attainable.

To illustrate further the process of working on a manageable task, let me recall a rare occasion when I was home for an entire autumn weekend. My vision was to spend a couple hours raking and burning leaves. Weeks before, I had raked leaves into a large pile and covered them with a tarp for protection from the rain. The weekend I found myself home, I pulled off the tarp, raked up another wheelbarrow full of newly fallen leaves, and added those new leaves to the pile. A second wheelbarrow-full did the trick and I was ready to get the matches, a shovel, and nearby hose in case the fire got too large.

I struck matches and put them under the dry

leaves at various places on the pile. Smoke and fire started up slowly, but then the fire smoldered out. I struck more matches, holding each matchstick under the leaves. Then I tried stirring up the leaves to provide air. Only then did I see that the leaves left under the tarp were damp and dense. I took a shovel and mixed the dry leaves into the wet ones, hoping that when they caught, they would provide the necessary heat to dry out the wet leaves.

Several smoky sections had a glimpse of a spark, but otherwise little flame. I went into the house and searched for some lamp oil, drenched a piece of cardboard, tore it into several pieces to create "wicks," and placed them strategically around the pile of leaves, determined now that I would succeed. There were wonderful flare-ups and a whole section caught fire. Aha! This is going to work, I thought. One section in particular looked promising. I piled more leaves onto it to provide fuel, only to smother that section as well.

The pile was smoking and smoldering, but burning was not happening. What else could I try? A few more attempts at lighting the dry leaves helped start another section, but then it fizzled out as well. The reality was that the wet leaves were too difficult to burn, regardless of my attempts. I decided to let die whatever sparks were left, cover the pile with the tarp, and renew my efforts in the spring.

This story exemplifies what constitutes a combination of effort, ability, manageability, and success. My efforts were contained in the striking of matches, the mixing of dry and wet leaves, and providing the oil-soaked cardboard wicks. Certainly I have the ability to start a pile of leaves on fire. And the more effort I applied engaging that ability, the more likely they would light. Except that I was not successful, because the leaves were wet; the task was not a manageable one. And, frankly, I wasted a lot of valuable home time!

Had I broken the task down to manageable steps, I might have taken some of the leaves to form smaller piles. I could have allowed them to dry in the sun for an hour or so. I could have doused them with lamp oil, allowing one small pile to burn and then adding to it until all the leaves were successfully burned. Or, I could have put them in a bag and delivered them to the composting area at the recycling center!

More importantly, had I enlisted the support of a coach, he or she would have provided feedback on my efforts. More knowledge might have reduced the amount of effort I exerted. In a recent book about UCLA basketball coach John Wooden, *You Haven't Taught Until They Have Learned*, who has ten national championships, it is revealed that Wooden's comments during practice did not consist of praise or criticism but of giving information. Knowledge increased the payoff players received from their efforts more than any other feedback, and thus motivated more effort. Harkening back to Chapter 3, working from one's strengths and then adding knowledge further motivates increased effort.

Given my desire to stay at home and burn the leaves with what I had, my efforts were good ones. My ability remained intact, and I acknowledged that the initial task of burning a huge pile of wet leaves was not a manageable one and needed to be broken down into tasks that allowed for more of a payoff. A coach might have allowed me to arrive at that conclusion earlier and/or provided information to make the event a successful one.

My leaf-burning project demonstrates the necessity of chunking down a large project into manageable tasks. It also shows that, once aware of the process, I can take ownership of my efforts and abilities. Had I done so early on, I would not have expended needless effort toward an unattainable task. Students who understand how the components of achieving success work together remain motivated by their efforts, knowing that taking one step at a time might be the better course of action.

In previous chapters, we've looked at the power of vision and belief to achieve success. Yet without a manageable task, belief soon erodes, as success becomes elusive. Coaches have long understood the power of assigning a task to the player that matches or slightly exceeds his or her abilities in order to maximize the payoff or result of the effort expended. Once one task is achieved, increased motivation spurs the student on to the next challenge.

Seeing the end result broken down into manageable tasks allows a motivated learner to master each task, moving closer to success and, therefore, feeding motivation again, in ever-increasing movement toward successful results. Those who can't break the ultimate success into manageable tasks become overwhelmed and lose motivation. As educators, we need to look at a student's abilities and the success we want him or her to achieve, and help steer effort into tasks that are manageable.

The film *Rudy* focuses on a boy whose vision, dream, and belief center upon playing football for Notre Dame University. His ability to see the enormity of his desire broken into manageable tasks constitutes the theme of the movie. As a young high school student, Rudy's financial situation doesn't even come close to the ability to afford to go to college, much less to Notre Dame. Manageable Task #1: Rudy gets a job.

In addition to his financial problems, Rudy's grade point average precludes his entering Notre Dame. Manageable Task #2: Rudy attends a neighboring school, applies effort, and makes his grades acceptable to Notre Dame. On the football field, Rudy works out, practices, and studies all the plays, but he's ultimately not invited onto the squad. Manageable Task #3: Get onto the practice team first.

The movie ends with Rudy playing football for Notre Dame, the crowd cheering, success achieved.

There are countless stories such as Rudy's. Each involves people motivated sufficiently to apply effort in ways that result in success. My own dream is that more students capture the motivation that inspires the Rudys, the Rockys, the James Earl Joneses, the Lance Armstrongs, or any other hero or successful leader. We spend so much school time meeting standards and ticking off subject matter that the process of learning—the sheer joy of achieving a task with only a little more effort—oftentimes gets lost. And if that's the case, then what's the point? We are like the tribesmen in the Introduction of this book, hopelessly dousing a burning roof without the right tools.

WeightWatchers, one of the most successful international weight loss programs, understands the value not only of effort, but of celebrating successes achieved with manageable tasks. People join WeightWatchers and often lose 30, 40, 80, even 100 pounds. But not on the first day. Those desiring substantial weight loss are advised to start with ten pounds; many share in testimonials that they lost their 80 pounds ten at a time.

Following the WeightWatchers program (making the effort) allows members to achieve their goals one pound or ten pounds at a time. At WeightWatchers meetings, hands are raised for people having lost up to a pound, two pounds, four or more, etc. Each time, their efforts are literally applauded. At five pounds, they receive a bookmark to indicate success at that manageable task. Stars are applied to the bookmark for each additional five-pound loss. Grown men and women eagerly raise their hands to claim these stars, charms, key rings, and other rewards signifying various levels of achievement. And as they apply their effort toward reducing food intake or exercising or counting their points, their ability to do so multiplies.

The WeightWatchers program might well serve as a model for classroom goals. As each manageable task is completed through applied effort (which then multiplies ability), success is rewarded. Good teachers implement this concept by providing students with manageable tasks to achieve success. My point is that we need to isolate these steps to reinforce for students the value of effort toward ultimate success. And the in-between step is often the manageable task that makes the final picture not seem so daunting.

Here's an excerpt from educator Chick Moorman's book *Spirit Whisperers: Teachers Who Nourish a Child's Spirit* that shows how teachers may look at tasks as insurmountable ("That sounds like a lot of work!") until they break them down into manageable steps:

Skywalker Sprouts, Inc. is a business. It is owned and operated by 25 second graders and their teacher, Sally Rutherford (not her real name), at an elementary school in a metropolitan area in Michigan.

The sprout business germinated in Sally's mind during the summer. "I've always shied away from organizing a business in the classroom," she told me, "because I felt I couldn't make the time commitment. We are under so much pressure to raise the test scores that anything fun, interesting, or demanding a degree of internal motivation is frowned upon by the administration."

But Sally raised sprouts for her family during the summer and enjoyed the experience. "I came to see sprouts as an easy process," she says, "and it creates a nice product. And I am a professional educator. I know I have to get these students involved if learning is going to stick for any length of time beyond the testing period."

The simplicity of the project was tempting, but would the students enjoy sprouts? Sally decided to check it out. During one of her traditional afternoon fruit breaks, she substituted sprouts for the fruit. The children enjoyed them and Skywalker Sprouts moved closer to existence.

With the students' taste and interest tested, Sally moved ahead with her plan. A shopping committee was given the task of purchasing supplies. Alfalfa seeds, bought at a local health food store, cost $2.19 a pound. Gallon jars and baggies required an additional expenditure. Sally supplied the front money and the business started to grow.

A typical sprout harvest lasts one week. Sally begins by soaking the seeds at home on Saturday night. On Monday, she transports the swollen seeds to school, where students put them in gallon jars. Cheesecloth is then placed over the jar openings and secured. Students thoroughly rinse the seeds and spread them around three or four times a day. On the second day, roots appear. Leaves sprout on the third or fourth day. On Thursday, the sprouts are placed under a light source so they will "green up."

On Friday the sprouts are readied for marketing. Students bag them in three-ounce portions. In assembly line fashion, the seven- and eight-year-olds weigh, bag, staple, and box the sprouts. Orders taken on Monday are then filled. Money is collected, counted, and banked.

Initial selling was limited to parents of Skywalker students. Two one-gallon jars were necessary to fill the demand. More recent selling has involved the entire school. Now five one-gallon jars are in operation. Students rotate jobs every three weeks. Applicants must fill out a form indicating their preferred job, experience, and reasons for applying. Jobs include label maker, cashier, bookkeeper, rinser, cleanup, packager, delivery person, and advertiser. Everyone participates each week.

So far, the project has been a success. Parents report using and enjoying the sprouts. Children have been observed choosing sprouts over candy during school parties. The class has developed a heightened sense of group pride and togetherness.

As with any business, problems and frustrations exist. What do you do with excess crop if all the sprouts are not sold? How do you handle crop failure? How do you explain to prepaid customers you can't fill their orders because of a broken jar?

Yet, problems breed opportunity. When problems arise, students get to experience the solution-seeking process firsthand. They have real opportunities to practice problem solving and overcoming adversity. They get to practice planning, cooperating, and working together to reach a common goal.

A booklet on sprouts was produced by Skywalker for distribution to first-time customers. It details some basic facts about sprouts, lists recipes, and describes the sprout-growing process. On page four of that booklet, one second grader wrote, "You soak them in jars. And you rinse them many times a day until Friday. Then you sell them."

While initially the great idea of creating a business in the classroom seemed like an overwhelming task to Sally, she started with small steps, checking the pulse of her students' interest, introducing one aspect at a time. As the students began to apply their effort toward making sprouts, seeing the reward in selling (and eating) them, they took on more and more ownership and responsibility for the business. Each took on a task; all benefited. Sally completed her vision, one little sprout at a time.[2]

As educators, we know to build a snowman. A child must first make a round snowball and roll it through the snow, adding more and more to it to create a large ball and a strong base. That effort repeats with two other round balls similarly created. Once the three are propped one on top of the other, the child creates features—pebbles for eyes, a stick for a nose, or other features the child may design. Each step requires effort that increases their ability (it's far easier to do the middle ball than it was to do the first because the child's effort on the first increased his or her ability). Each step furthers the process toward the end result and thus motivates achievement.

But suppose as an educator you were teaching "Snowman," and one child could hardly get his or her hands (or mind) around the concept of the first snowball and another student jumped up and easily built the snowman, eventually creating an elegant snow sculpture? How do you teach "Snowman" to both students? Enter differentiated instruction, the topic of our next chapter.

[2] From *Spirit Whisperers: Teachers Who Nourish a Child's Spirit* by Chick Moorman. Reprinted with permission. Copyright © 2001 Chick Moorman and Personal Power Press. www.chickmoorman.com

Chapter 5:
Differentiated Success

Formulas are predictable; kids are not. Applying effort to multiply ability when applied to a manageable task will result in success.

$$\frac{\text{EFFORT} \times Ability + \text{Manageable Task}}{\text{BELIEF} \quad \text{VISION}} = \textbf{SUCCESS!}$$

What constitutes a manageable task for one student might be a huge challenge for another. This is particularly so as classrooms come to include a wider array of cultures, languages, ages, and socioeconomic backgrounds. When we add to that the need to provide each student with adequate yearly progress (AYP), the challenge teachers face in devising multiple levels of learning becomes apparent.

Special Education teachers have long known the need and value of modifying instruction so students see a payoff for efforts made. Coaches know this too. In sports, gain in ability only occurs when the practice undertaken by players is challenging and feasible for the individual.

If a team went to the weight room to work out (or if you or I were working out at a gym), the coach or trainer would not expect everyone to be lifting the same weight. A newcomer to the gym or a weaker student who struggles at lifting a heavy weight wastes effort. Lighter weights with an appropriate number of repetitions would be necessary in order to build ability and strength.

Students for whom the current weight represents no effort at all would need to have the coach make adjustments in the workout routine. As for the local gym, working out with the same weight or machine week after week without upping the ante would not increase the member's strength or ability, just maintain the status symbol ("Oh, yeah, I work out every day"). Right.

Assessment

Varying instruction to meet each student's needs has a solid place in the classroom. Assessing the skill level of students becomes crucial to achieve this. Teachers need to take time to discover—and value—what students bring into the classroom and build on that.

Recalling the strengths-based and Appreciative Inquiry approach discussed in Chapter 3, educators can focus on the strengths of students to assist them in achieving their vision of success. Different strengths, different visions exist throughout the classroom. Educators who modify tasks to suit the strengths and skill levels of their students achieve more results than those who assume each student arrives at the task in the same way. And this also makes the learning relevant, which substantially drives motivation, as we will see in Chapter 8.

It is unlikely that teachers can design an individualized lesson plan for each student. Yet there tend to be skill levels into which several students fall, and some basic assessment tools—including simple questions or student demonstrations—can quickly give the teacher a handle on the makeup of the classroom. As a teacher works with students on tasks, the differences become more apparent.

When approaching a unit of study, a teacher can model what is expected of students. To cover the fact that some "already know this," the teacher can reinforce learning by pointing to it and adding, "as you know," or "as some of you have figured out." Even if students claim they know a skill, repeating it reinforces it. While the teacher teaches the material, it is information being reinforced by one group, learned anew by a second group, and finally sinking in for another group who may have heard it before but were not ready for it then.

This reminds me of lines from the video *Fish! Catch the Energy, Release the Potential* about the Pike's Place Fish Market in Seattle. The manager remarks that, at one time, he used to roll his eyes every time a customer asked a question, because it was the same question that someone had just asked him ten minutes before. Yet the manager had to acknowledge to himself that the person asking the question now was genuinely interested and did not even know the person who had asked the same question earlier. In the same way, a teacher can state information, and at the next class period—or even in the same class period—may hear students ask a question about it, as if the information were never given. Eyes could be rolled, but if truth be told, even if the student heard the information before, he or she was not aware of it at the time or did not relate to its meaning. It did not compute. Not a big deal, really. Repeat the same information, just as the fish market manager answered the question again.

Modeling and sharing expectations with students allows those who think they know to deepen their knowledge. Putting a sentence on the board and adding punctuation while pointing out why the periods or commas are there might achieve an "Aha" from one student, and an "Oh, yeah. I remember that!" from another, and a "Huh?" from yet another.

One of my favorite examples of varying or differentiating instruction comes from David Bordenkircher, principal at South Lake High School in Lake County, FL who served as band director for many years. Bordenkircher reminds us that while, to the audience, a concert appears to be one piece of music—one product—it actually consists of a labyrinth of varying musical levels. Yet the goal or standard put forth to the students in the band was to achieve good sound quality, regardless of the level of playing.

Bordenkircher assigned different musical parts

to students that reflected their abilities, which he determined through preassessment, listening, and having students audition for various "chairs" that make up a band or orchestra (1st trumpet, 2nd trumpet, etc.). Some had technical skills down pat—the correct notes, right rhythm, in sync with others, timing. Others expressed musicality- good tone, clear sound, pacing, and emotion. The musicians' skill levels varied widely, yet they built a performance and achieved a musical product because the director differentiated the tasks.

Music publishers provide several levels and parts for each musical instrument, with different levels of technical requirements. Some include complex rhythms or high notes requiring technical abilities in wind instruments, for example, and those Bordenkircher assigned to students who could be challenged by them and succeed (fulfill their vision). Other musical selections called for tones at lower range and not much demand for rhythm, and these were assigned to students developing their musical abilities. Bordenkircher made sure each selection was challenging to the student—requiring them to exert the effort to stretch, to learn, and to play at their highest and best level, regardless of where that was in the spectrum.

The students improved through daily practice as they were given instruction on playing technique and musicality, each within his or her level of playing. Yet they also had to learn to work together. To illustrate his point, Bordenkircher typically mentioned the nicest car driven by one of the students and told the class they were going to go outside and take this car apart, throwing all the pieces into the middle of the parking lot. He said whoever could start the pile of car parts could have the car.

His point was that each musician had to be aware of what was going on in the other parts of the music in order for it to work. Rhythms needed to synchronize. The sounds had to appear to be congruent. Players needed to understand the other parts. He challenged students at all levels to apply effort. And, though he had the advantage of music publishers' providing for varying levels of skill in the music books, there is nothing that says educators cannot take one text book and provide different parts to match the skill and interest level of students.

Another type of differentiated instruction involves creating ways to bring a student up to par when he or she may be lacking necessary skills for one reason or another. For example, a middle school social studies teacher finds one or two of her students cannot read as well as others. These students muddled through classes prior to hers without developing good reading skills. If reading was missed, the student needs to pick it up as he or she goes along and/or obtain reading assistance. Because our teacher has to cover the social studies curriculum, she cannot take the time to teach these students to read.

Rather, she varies her approach to the social studies curriculum to assist students in gaining content, even if reading may only improve slightly. The teacher may develop a study guide. She could ask students to take turns making an audiotape of the chapter being covered, reading it aloud. Creating a class play, where everyone knows the lines and some fill in for other actors, is another option. Students could partner up and one could read the chapter aloud while the other takes notes. It can be a very creative process for the teacher inspired to do whatever it takes to teach social studies, even if it requires varying the instruction to meet each student's needs.

John Schmitt, an Advanced Placement and Honors Psychology teacher at McDowell High School in Erie, PA, admitted he goes so far as to offer D and F students the option of taking a test over if they were not satisfied with their grade. "Some students' brains aren't wired for test taking," says Schmitt. "Why not give them another opportunity?" Eventually B and C students wanted a shot at improving their score through additional effort too. Since Schmitt typically makes up several versions of a test, the chances of their taking the exact test over were slim, and he says it was easy to identify anyone who cheated.

Students retaking the test were responsible for studying the material and returning at a time and place that accommodated Schmitt's schedule, not the other way around. This option falls into the category of varying the instruction, as it allows students who want to excel the opportunity to apply more effort by studying, thereby accelerating their abilities and knowledge of the material. It also *provides an option* and *places responsibility,* two tenets of brain-based learning we'll explore in Chapters 7 and 8.

At opposite ends of the spectrum are students who can practically write novels sitting next to those who are still learning sentence structure. Educators need to look at the purpose and goal for each child, and identify the effort that best moves toward that goal. For the child needing to write a sentence, the focus is narrow and specific—basic sentence, no frills. For the child who has tackled the basics of sentence structure, expand the challenge to a full page or even a short story.

The caution flag here involves students who claim, "We already *know* this stuff!" when in fact they may not. Students, particularly those in middle school and above, seldom cop to their inadequacies, so assessment by informal student survey often backfires. At the same time, teachers will not want to blow off the student's comments and give a basic unit test to those who really *do* know the "stuff," as that reinforces the school-is-so-boring syndrome that often leads to student dropout or at least downshifting.

The central message in a March 2006 report developed by Civic Enterprises in association with Peter D. Hart Research Associates for the Bill & Melinda Gates Foundation called "The Silent Epidemic: Perspectives of High School Dropouts," was that most dropouts were students who could have succeeded—and believed they could have succeeded—in school had they stayed. Forty-seven percent attributed dropping out mainly to uninteresting classes. Most said they were bored or disengaged.

More to the point of effort, 69 percent of drop out students surveyed said they were not motivated or inspired to work hard—apply effort—and two-thirds of these students claimed they would have worked harder if more were demanded of them. Seventy percent admitted they were confident they could have graduated if they had tried.

In differentiated instruction, "learning contracts" can be developed between teacher and student to cover whatever goals, tasks, or knowledge the student plans to achieve. (Such contracts are covered in the PLS course *Differentiated Instruction for Today's Classrooms*™.) If a student claims he or she "already knows this," the teacher can give that student the test, and, if he or she scores 90 percent correct or better, then that test is folded into the learning contract. Additional work on the unit, covering another aspect they want to study, becomes part of their learning plan.

For example, if a student says he knows the basic information on the Civil War, he can take the unit test and, scoring well, can then move on to the politics or economics or slavery or some other aspect of the Civil War unit that interests him. He does this parallel to those in the class who continue to study what he has proven he already knows. He is simply applying more effort to that area of study because he already has shown he has ability in the other.

The task of learning basic Civil War information, being very manageable, eliminated any need for further effort. Augmenting the information with in-depth learning about a specific aspect for which he has interest (and which is therefore relevant) gives the student a manageable task, but one that carries with it some challenge (thus requiring effort), and remains focused on his goal (the learning contract). The teacher coaches or guides students differently depending on their strengths and their needs.

The most important element for breaking down instruction to meet varying needs, levels of knowledge, and interests is assessing where students are in the learning process. Next, make the prerequisites of any assignment or unit of study clear: break it down to manageable chunks. Then revise the rubric to make the learning more challenging or basic, depending on the needs. And, finally, something often missed in teaching: provide feedback. How did they do? Where are they in the plan to apply the effort? How well did they meet your expectation?

Feedback not only makes the student a part of the teaching/learning process (thus generating a sense of ownership and therefore meaning), but it also automatically adds a new layer of assessment to carry them forward to the next unit. Both the frequency and the immediacy of feedback are strongly associated with brain-based learning. We'll look more at the value of feedback in Chapter 6.

Learning Styles

There you are in the faculty lunchroom talking about the miraculous event wherein the school district sent a free computer to each teacher's home (yes, I know, another fantasy)! "Well, everyone told me it was the best brand," says Juanita, authoritatively. "I can't believe they sent it to me. It's so compact and smooth to the touch. I already had my desk set up for it, and it fit perfectly next to the plants. Later my friend George—he's a great guy, and a genius at computers—came by and walked me through using it. I just love it!"

"Well, good for you," responds Samuel. "My

computer doesn't seem to respond to anything I do unless I'm on the phone with tech support! I probably spend half my time talking to them instead of working on the computer. Hope the district didn't waste their money."

"Mine works great!" beams Jim. "I set it up and just jumped right into using it. Not sure what all it does," he adds, "But I'll bop around on it and find out."

"I'm still reading the instructions," adds Barbara.

Instructions? Someone reads computer instructions? Well, that would be a visual learner. What we are talking about here, of course, are learning styles. Juanita, with her desk set up and a friend coming to teach her, is a tactual learner. Samuel is obviously auditory and Jim, kinesthetic. And those are just the sensory preferences.

I use a tremendously valuable learning styles instrument developed by Performance Learning Systems, Inc.® called The Kaleidoscope Profile®. This profile combines three well-researched and documented surveys into one, and it is easy to administer to others—or yourself—with immediate and amazingly accurate results. Not only does it uncover sensory preferences, but also perceptual and organizational preferences and the temperament types for students, educators, and other adults in the workplace. It's available in print (with colorful stickers) or online at www.plsweb.com. (Click "The Kaleidoscope Profile" under "Resources for Teachers.")

When delivering instruction, of course, we need to be aware of and accommodate various learning styles. Rotating the delivery to include auditory, visual, tactual, and kinesthetic learners remains paramount in teaching, yet we often forget the dire need of students to pick up on the learning channel that suits *their* individual style. Of all high school dropouts, 80 percent are kinesthetic learners. Schools have not been conducive to kinesthetic or tactual learners—the latter requiring enriched environments, lots of activity, and a warm, comfortable setting if they are to learn. With schools across the country in disrepair and others with bars on the windows, the learning of tactual, kinesthetic, and visual students is at risk.

Certainly good teaching necessitates lessons and assignments that allow students both abstract and concrete experiences, global and sequential directions and presentations. Students need to be allowed, variously, to work at the board, walk around the room reciting; play physical games that sink in learning; read aloud, form discussion groups; read, see demonstrations, and work with graphics; or create a workspace and cooperative learning relationships in the classroom—learning to match all styles.

I recently had the opportunity to work with more than 10,000 middle and high school students who had completed The Kaleidoscope Profile. From the size and scope of this program, I was stunned to realize most of these students did not know how to study. Yet I shouldn't have been so surprised. I recalled I had only discovered the concept of studying toward the end of high school. I was walking down the hall one day and noticed my buddy Richie sitting on a bench reading. I yelled, "Hey Richie! What are you doing?" He said "Studying." Well, that threw me, as we were in the same class together. "Studying what?" I shot back. "'We didn't have an assignment today."

As I approached him, I saw he was rereading a chapter we had finished earlier. It was at that point I realized there were students going home and reviewing material teachers had not assigned. There was more to studying than simply completing an assignment. Some kids did it to learn more! If there was ever a class about how to study, I certainly missed it and, apparently, so had the 10,000 middle and high school Kaleidoscope students I worked with. I was amazed that nothing much had changed in the way teachers taught to reach a student's learning style—particularly how students could study in ways that matched their individual learning strengths.

Many teachers complain that students do not study; yet it is also true that many school programs do not have guidelines or classes in which to learn *how* to study. Part of knowing how to study involves empowering students to discover their preferred learning styles—their strengths—so they can study in that manner. Studying in a student's preferred style yields the greatest payoff for the time and effort invested.

A kinesthetic high school male, for example, should avoid staying after school to study in the library with his visual girlfriend. This is hard for a virile high school male to accept, but it just won't work. While his girlfriend will actually study, he will probably sharpen his pencil 12 times. She will do well on the test, and he will not, thus reinforcing the belief that studying isn't worthwhile.

Instead, our kinesthetic high school guy should go home, put his vocabulary words on index cards— words on one side, definitions on the other. He should lay the index cards on the driveway and dribble his basketball to each card, pick it up, read the definition, and recall the word. When he can dribble and answer the whole stack without having to flip the cards over, he'll know he's ready for the test. And then he can call his girlfriend.

Likewise, a student who is highly visual and not strongly auditory probably would do best not to study with a friend. It would be better to study first (read and look at the material) and *then* visit with the friend. Auditory and tactual students would benefit by joining a study group. A highly tactual student will probably find it better to study in the kitchen while there is family commotion, cooking aromas, and warmth rather than tucked in a metal desk somewhere in her bedroom. The visual learner may prefer studying alone in his or her bedroom.

A student with a global preference, who requires the big picture, might do well to see a timeline, map or flow chart instead of reading three sequential chapters on the subject. The abstract global student might also want to understand the meaning of what he or she is studying—what's the overall point? Satisfying his or her intuitive grasp would then allow settling into the sequential reading, knowing where it was going and why.

A concrete-sequential learner might want to have the steps lined up for him or her before proceeding—perhaps be able to leaf through whatever class materials are available from the teacher's lesson plan—in order to understand, to "touch and feel" the content.

And so on. The point underscored here is that differentiated instruction cannot exist unless there is some attention paid to the students' learning styles. Certainly anyone can learn in any modality. But why not improve the chances and the effort by using the innate strength—the preferred style—to augment the effort and the ability and the ultimate success? Don't know a student's preferred style? Although administering a learning-styles survey presents the best method, there are other ways to determine the style.

Bill Haggart has written a wonderful book called *Homework and Kids: A Parent's Guide* wherein he provides a guide for detecting and understanding student and parent styles. Beyond that, the book packs in numerous effective and fun ways students can accomplish homework in their preferred styles.

Generational Differences

While not as finitely quantified and documented as learning style modalities, the real differences among generations cannot be ignored. For the first time in history, there are now four distinct generations working and learning side-by-side every day. Each carries its own set of values, influences, history, and relationship to technology. Each generation also has its own system of rewards and preferred types of acknowledgment and feedback.

Unlike learning style differences among students, generational difference occurs between student and

Generational Differences

Traditionalists	Baby Boomers	Generation X	Millennials
Born 1900-1945 (75 million)	Born 1946-1964 (80 million)	Born 1965-1980 (46 million)	Born 1981-1999 (76 million)
Value: Institutions Loyalty	Value: Change Optimism Competition	Value New Ideas Resourcefulness Skepticism of institutions	Value: Realism Work that makes a difference
		Raised as technology blossomed	Always have known technology

Figure 5.1

teacher, with the teacher bringing a value system that differs from his or her students. This new layer of differentiation between teacher and students mandates some self-understanding on the part of the teacher.

Depending upon which demographic study you review, generally students born from 1982 to 2005 comprise what is called the Millennial Generation (or Generation Y or the Echo Boom), as many are children of Baby Boomers born 1946 to 1964. While Baby Boomers numbering 80 million have long reigned in our society as the largest demographic bulge, experiencing substantial social and cultural changes all their lives, Millennials, just behind them numerically at 76 million, have an impact of their own.

Generation Xers were born from approximately 1965 to 1980 and number 46 million people. They were the first to experience technology in their lives on a daily basis. They are the ones in hot demand by tech companies, as demand exceeds the supply of those with their talents. Millennials, showing up after 1980, have experienced technology in their bedrooms, the palms of their hands, and certainly on television 24/7 *all* their lives. They have seen it all, including all the disasters. The values and influences of the Millennial generation have an impact on how they view learning. They have a more global view, and schools, studying, teaching, and its application appear to them in a perspective entirely different than that of their teachers, whether of Generation X or Baby Boomer. Traditionalists also work in schools, whether as administrators or retired teachers returning to the fold. These people, born before World War II, bring a wealth of value and insights possibly never learned by the Millennial generation.

The perspective that includes "Hey, I'll just check it out on the Web," does have implications in the classroom. For starters, anyone can contribute to the Web, so research seems to take a back seat. Millennials also completely understand and act on the choice provided by the Internet—an extremely brain-based medium, which is a good part of its wide appeal. They live in a world that opts for collaboration over competition, so sharing ideas and even discussing possible answers may have a greater appeal than test taking and competition.

There is a story about a manager in a high-tech company who wanted his next level middle managers to come up with a solution to a technical problem being experienced by the company (think teacher presenting a complicated problem for students to solve). He offered it as a challenge and hinted that the winning solution might lead to a promotion or be acknowledged in some way (think Donald Trump as he challenged his protégés on the television reality show *The Apprentice*).

To his surprise, the Millennial middle managers, then in their late 20s and early 30s, ended up emailing one another and collaborated fiercely, enjoying the interaction and the problem solving. They actually did not care about the promotion, since Millennials have seen too often how those at the top can tumble, and achieving great fame and fortune does not necessarily carry with it rewards. If anything, Millennials echo their Boomer parents' social interests, and many would rather work toward saving the planet than drilling for oil in the corporate model.

Certainly generational differences in the classroom represent another difference, albeit one between student and educators or administrators in the school. Another aspect of differentiating instruction— to provide manageable tasks—falls right behind meeting a student's learning style and skill level. But varying instruction for manageability should also take into account the students' beliefs and values.

Finally, differentiation of "instruction" may require keen awareness, caring, and an unusual approach on the part of the teacher. Professional Development Specialist Penny Jadwin of Lynn Haven, FL shares the story of Antoinette, a girl of five whom Jadwin had the pleasure of assisting while doubling as teacher and head of the special education department at the school district where she worked at the time.

Jadwin noticed Antoinette on the first day of school. She was excited, smiling, her braids pumping up and down. Every day over the next month, however, Jadwin watch Antoinette's behavior change from an excited, energetic, loving girl to a child her mother had to push and drag into the classroom.

One day Jadwin received a copy of Antoinette's papers on her desk in her capacity as head of special ed. The report stated Antoinette had ceased to talk in her classroom. Jadwin, an auditory learner and now a presenter found not talking to be very odd behavior. "It takes a lot of power not to talk," she said, "especially for a five year old."

The report stated Antoinette was labeled "Elective Mute" and that was the end of any further action. Jadwin couldn't keep the happy little girl she had seen out of her mind, so she did some research and learned that Antoinette did, in fact, have a slight speech problem. She also learned Antoinette was from Arkansas, and she was in a classroom with a teacher from Mississippi. Despite the states' proximity, their accents were and are distinctly different. Whenever Antoinette had spoken, as it turned out, the teacher corrected her. Between the differing accents and Antoinette's speech problem, the teacher ended up constantly correcting her—in reality, *over*-correcting her to the point that Antoinette just stopped talking all together.

Jadwin had the child transferred to her classroom, where it took months of positive interaction to build trust with Antoinette. She asked Antoinette to communicate with her in drawings, a manageable task that, when Jadwin responded, lent celebration to Antoinette's efforts. She encouraged her, interacted with her, building the nonverbal communication and trust. Antoinette was not mentally handicapped or learning disabled; she simply had a minor speech problem and a bigger problem of being affected by over-correction.

The breakthrough came when Jadwin gave Antoinette full responsibility for taking care of the classroom guinea pig. Antoinette would come to Jadwin to let her know when the guinea pig needed something. While she would respond to Antoinette's methods of communication about the guinea pig, Jadwin was working to find the teachable moment, to test the trust level. She often responded to Antoinette with questions, "I don't understand. What does the guinea pig need? I'm not sure I know what you're trying to tell me, Antoinette? What does she need?"

Finally, almost in Helen Keller fashion, Antoinette blurted out, "Water. He needs more water!"

Lesson? We often make judgments and quickly squelch students' efforts, and we bypass opportunities to simply use the tools of assessment, learning style, creative ways to differentiate instruction, a nod to generational differences, and finally giving students—all students—the benefit of the doubt. Take time to find out what they can do, and then tailor your instruction to meet with that talent.

Chapter 6:
Encouraging Success

All this talk about effort may be well and good, you might say, but how do we motivate students to make an effort? How do we help them understand that, with effort, there is a big payoff, whether they're college bound or not?

Finding ways to encourage and motivate students poses a problem particularly when teachers have not had a chance to know their students. In my book *Quality Teaching in a Culture of Coaching,* we emphasize coaches getting to know their coachees by learning about their visions and beliefs in order to be most effective in coaching them. We also look at ways teachers in large high schools may work with other coaches and teachers to get to know students better.

While we may not be able to motivate each and every student individually, in this and subsequent chapters we will look at the importance of an encouraging environment, motivating strategies, and the myriad ways we can empower, enliven, and set a fire under students to achieve their vision and, yes, have fun as they exert the effort to do so.

Encouragement

To generate any kind of learning, an encouraging learning environment must be in place. While most teachers are well aware of this as demonstrated by their magical and enlivened classrooms, it is also important to communicate—to say and do things that reinforce and encourage student effort.

Positive feedback in and of itself increases intrinsic motivation (Ryan & Deci, 2000). Feedback expressed in ways that encourages future effort provides as much if not more extrinsic reward as other forms of tangible "goodies" designed to reward students for completing a task.

If effort is directly tied to a reward—give a little effort, get a little reward—the student often does not make the connection that it is his or her vision or belief of success that drives effort. Effort is an outgrowth of the belief in success that then increases ability. As a student recognizes effort as a tool—a means to an end—then he or she will be motivated to try again and the reward is real success and the satisfaction of having achieved it little by little.

Key to an encouraging learning environment is a focus on learning for understanding rather than working to memorize or perform—to complete Tasks A, B, and C. Unless a student wants another "goodie," his or her effort in the task-oriented learning environment remains out of context, a cog in a wheel, much like the Industrial Age and its carried-over view of "work."

Activist, educator, and author Alfie Kohn states in an article, "Students Don't 'Work'—They Learn: Our Use of Workplace Metaphors May Compromise the Essence of Schooling," that students, over time, have become more focused on achievement than on learning. When students are "put to work," he states:

"Tasks come to be seen as—indeed, are often explicitly presented as—means to an end. What counts is the number of right answers, although even this may be seen as just a prerequisite to snagging a good grade. In fact, the grade may be a means to making the honor roll, which, in turn, may lead to special privileges or rewards provided at school or at home. With each additional inducement, the original act of learning is further devalued."

Perspective

Kohn brings up an important point about perspective. Perspective, or a person's point of view, is used extensively in professional coaching. How we perceive things, how we frame them and then communicate from our own perspective has a tremendous impact on students—and vice versa. Teaching students perspective spells the difference between their identifying with a worker-bee mentality—"just tell me what I have to do and I'll do it"—to one of choosing the perspective that serves their vision, to achieve success.

To understand perspective concretely, imagine right now that a large, gray elephant walks into where you are reading this book. The elephant comes straight toward you and stops. You look up and see his large floppy ears, his fascinating trunk. You look into his soft eyes and watch mesmerized as he sweeps up hay into his mouth with his trunk. "What a fascinating creature," you think, smiling.

Now you get up and walk to the side of the elephant. He stands there quietly, and you realize how immense he is. You look at his leathery skin and down to his feet, which you see with alarm, are measured in feet, not inches. The elephant begins to sway slightly, and lifts up his back leg slightly. Suddenly you feel afraid. This animal is huge! You realize the weight of his foot could crush you, or the swaying movement may break down the floor he's standing on. "I'm afraid," you may say.

Finally, you go to the rear of the elephant and notice his drooping bottom and long, skinny tail. Staring at his hindquarters, you can't help but notice he wasn't very meticulous in the bathroom department, and this animal repulses you. "He's disgusting," you conclude.

Each of these visions of the elephant represents a different perspective, and from those perspectives, you will communicate differently. Likewise, when students are engaged in learning, the perspective of "work hard" or "see if you can't make an effort" varies greatly from one characterized by speaking with encouragement.

The value of perspective lies in recognizing which perspective—which view of the elephant—serves best to motivate you or your student to do the next positive thing. If a student is told to work out a math problem and the student sees it as being "sooooo haarrrrddd," that perspective doesn't serve him or her well. That's the back of the elephant.

A better perspective might be to first, simply change the language to "see if you can tackle at least the beginning of this problem"; and next, place the completion of the math problem within the context of the student's desire to achieve a certain goal. "When you finish this math problem, you will have completed the unit."

Words and phrases directly reflect a perspective, and once aware of those that do not serve to further a positive approach, achieve success, or feel better about a situation, one can simply change the words or phrases to create a perspective that becomes more positive, useful, "manageable." As an example, what teacher doesn't say from time to time, "I'm over-whelmed." (Have you ever met anyone *under*whelmed?) To change the feelings and the perspective of having so much to do, the pressure of time, the sense of being "overwhelmed," simply replacing the word with "challenged" seems to lighten things up. "I am feeling very challenged." "I am sure in demand these days!"

Likewise students who say they feel "stupid" reveal a perspective about themselves and their effort that does nothing to serve them. A switch to a better word to describe what they're feeling might simply be, "I'm still learning." Or "I'm discovering things and I'm not sure what they will be."

Encouraging Environment

A positive perspective thrives in an encouraging learning environment. This is an environment where students have the perspective that learning can be both challenging and fun—the focus is on that type of learning. Thinking is important. That's what we do in learning. In an encouraging learning environment, teachers believe students are capable of and responsible for learning.

Students help and respect one another, and each knows it is all right to have a different "manageable" task than someone else. Effort receives positive reinforcement and reward. Those applying effort to a manageable task are engaged in learning and receive coaching, encouragement, support, and advancement toward their vision, their goal, with a teacher identifying and reinforcing the success they achieved.

Communication in an encouraging environment generally focuses on the process. "Your *hard work* really shows in this project." "That math problem *was* a hard one! Let's do another to see if we can *make the formula work* this time." "Have you thought about the *next step* in this project?"

Discouraging Environment

In a discouraging environment, the focus is on work. There are tasks to be done. The teacher states what those tasks are and it is the teacher who takes responsibility for learning and evaluation. The perspective of the teacher focuses on negative expectations and beliefs about student capabilities. The students are reinforced by a system of punishment and rewards; for example, students may not go out to recess until their work is finished.

As in a business where high-controlling micro-management causes employees to downshift—not caring if they will advance or not—and become less productive, students who perceive their teachers as controlling without constructive, encouraging feedback tend to demonstrate lower motivation in the classroom (Noels, Clement, & Pelletier, 1999).

Again citing Alfie Kohn in his article "Students Don't "Work'—They Learn,"[1]

> *"Importing nomenclature of the workplace is something most of us do without thinking—which is in itself a good reason to reflect on the practice. Every time we talk about "homework" or "seat work" or "work habits," every time we describe the improvements in, or assessment of, a student's "work" in class, every time we urge children to "get to work" or even refer to "classroom management," we are using a metaphor with profound implication for the nature of schooling. In effect, we are equating what children do to figure things out with what adults do in offices and factories to earn money."*

In other words, we send misleading messages when we discuss learning with words that really belong in the workplace. It equates the two when, in fact, learning is a process that occurs separate from work or other endeavors. The implication should be that learning is fun, adventurous, and valuable

[1] "Students Don't Work—They Learn" by Alfie Kohn, as first appeared in *Education Week* on September 3, 1997. Reprinted with permission from the author.

any time, not that it is the educational version of whatever we consider "work."

Communication in a discouraging learning environment includes statements that are critical, opinionated, or give advice. "I'm ready to give up on you," or "You should do it this way instead," or "Why are you always a slowpoke?" or "Everybody knows that" or "Boys don't cry" and finally "If you don't try harder, you are going to fail." And on the latter phrase, the teacher would probably be right. Words are powerful, and they reflect perspective that is easily picked up and stored as belief by students, whether they are aware they are doing so or not.

Encouraging Words

Obviously we want to remain in the perspective and the environment of an encouraging classroom. Encouragement motivates students to come out of negative situations—to shift their perspective. Encouragement provides support when a student collapses into feeling discouraged, frustrated, uncertain, or unable to move on. Learners who are working at peak effort or who need to sustain effort also need encouragement, as do those who are taking or considering taking a risk.

In the old ballad "Home on the Range," the lyrics say, "Where seldom is heard, a discouraging word, and the skies are not cloudy all day." A word here about communicating encouragement: Encouraging words and phrases do not judge the learner; they focus on the task, process, product or behavior in which the learner is engaged. They can take the form of a specific comment made by a teacher or a peer. It may be that the learner feels encouraged when someone else asks for his or her opinion or involves the learner in decision making, a form of empowerment we'll look at in Chapter 9.

Encouraging words speak to action, behavior, and process. Teachers can ask, "What needs to be done next?" or "How is it going?" or "What is needed for this?" They can reinforce the learning with "Keep at it!" "That's it! Good job." And they can ask a question combined with reinforcement, such as "I'll bet we can do this one another way. What do you think?" or "We've done some like this before. Can you tell me or show me the parts you remember?"

It takes so little, yet acknowledging the effort can do much to move water from 211 degrees of heat to boiling by adding that one more degree, 212 and on its way to creating real steam.

Evaluative Praise

Beyond encouraging words, teachers might want to give praise in an evaluative manner—evaluative praise. Whereas encouragement focuses on the *process* or product or task or behavior—the action—an evaluative praise focuses on the *person*. "You are always so *cooperative*. I like that!" "That's just *perfect.* Wow!" "Next time maybe you'll get *all* of them right! I'm sure you *can do it!*" "Of course I *expect* you to get an A. You're so *smart.*"

Evaluative praise addresses abilities and rewards effort well done by the student. It is teacher-centered, based on the teacher's values and standards, and it can be used in a manipulative way to express what is desired in a person, such as "I like the way Sally is standing in line quietly."

Praise in general can carry a double meaning. On the one hand it compliments, but it can also add pressure. "You're so smart—I know you can do it" carries with it the pressure to perform. And, it reflects more upon the person giving the praise—that person's values—than on the recipient. Praise also offers no specific feedback ("smart" is nonspecific) so could ring hollow.

Approval Statements

As in motivation, approval statements rely on some knowledge of what the learner values, and that means getting to know the student. You can easily pick up what a learner values in short order by paying attention to his or her actions, communication, and what he or she produces.

Credible, sincere, and believable approval feels the best to those receiving it. Labels tend not to be accepted, as they are a catchall. Approval statements are always based on what the recipient values (rather than what the giver of the approval values).

We react in interesting ways when it comes to compliments and praise. We often fidget, brush them off, become embarrassed, or say, "Aw, shucks," feeling we're not worthy. Approval statements focus on what we value and find worthwhile, so we are more apt to hear it without a negative reaction.

Guidelines when delivering approval statements include the need to first find what the person values; second, express the approval using adjectives that are positive and speak to the person's values (capable, honest, competent, creative, interesting, humorous, responsible, organized, polished, etc.); third, give the approval in one sentence; and then, fourth, shut up!

So often we give approval statements and then continue speaking without allowing the other person to truly get the approval. "Your project showed tremendous thought and creativity, *and* I know half the class was impressed." What? Only half?

Giving the approval statement and then keeping quiet to listen and observe allows you to pick up on body language and maintain eye contact with the student to make sure it landed correctly, which is yet another way of learning about your students' values. If you say, "Your project showed tremendous thought and creativity" and STOP, you can determine if he or she values thought and creativity by watching the student bask in the approval, smiling, eyes twinkling, pleased. Isn't this part of why we teach?

Figure 6.1, "Using an Encouraging Environment to Manage Learner Risk," is a graphic of these various responses by a teacher to encourage an environment of learning.

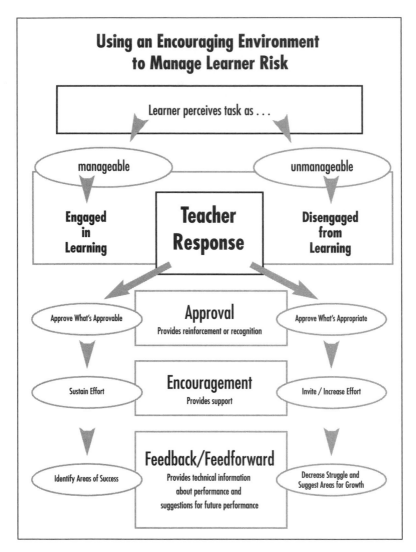

Figure 6.1

Feedback and Feedforward

While immediate and frequent feedback serves as one of the tenets of brain-based teaching and learning covered more thoroughly in Chapter 8, the concept of "feedforward" represents yet another way to shift the perspective to encourage and give approval to a student so that he or she wants to apply more effort to succeed.

Encouragement and well-delivered praise lets the student know you see and appreciate what he or she is doing, so the student will be more likely to include you in his or her vision, dreams, and efforts. The approval statement anchors the student's attention and thus creates an opportunity for further communication with you. It also focuses on the future: what's next? Feedback and feedforward statements move the student from where he or she is to future learning, which may be uncertain.

Feedback represents evidence you have gathered from others or from personal observations that tells the student about what happened in the past— what he or she did, the performance completed, and what progress he or she made (past tense) toward the goal.

Feedforward is present- or future-focused. It supplies the learner with ideas about what to do next. The key here as we look back to our manageable task discussion is that feedforward applies both to the student who is struggling to achieve and the one who is successful.

Together, Feedback and Feedforward represent an awesome combination. Feedback gives students a way to check progress toward goals, both short- and long-term. Feedforward clarifies the direction needed for improvement and gives students information about the learning they are engaged in so they can rekindle their efforts and use the feedforward information to succeed.

Feedforward serves as a motivational strategy as it focuses on the present and then future to move toward the vision. Feedback on past performance coupled with feedforward on what they are doing now and can do in the future shores up students' beliefs. This motivates additional effort, increased ability, and ultimate success.

Let's look at the illustration for Gordon's Ladder, Figure 6.2, to see how these statements might work to move a student from initial effort to success.

On the first rung of this ladder we see Jack with his kite. He has no idea what it is, what it does, or what he is expected to do with it. He is Unconsciously Unskilled. He does not know what he does not know. No effort is exerted from one who is unconsciously unskilled because he or she doesn't even know where to begin. Here a teacher or coach might first paint a picture, give him a vision. Next he or she might actually model what a kite can do so Jack begins to understand. The teacher can fly the kite so Jack can see it.

"Look, Jack. Once you learn how to fly this kite, you will be able to look up in the sky and see *your* beautiful kite sailing along, attached by a string to you!"

The teacher might add a belief. "Lots of people fly kites, Jack, and you are very athletic, so I know you can do it, don't you?"

On the next level, Jack has made some effort. He understands the concept of kite flying and he has tried to put the kite together properly to launch it. But now he is Consciously Unskilled. He knows what he doesn't know. He knows it will take effort to learn

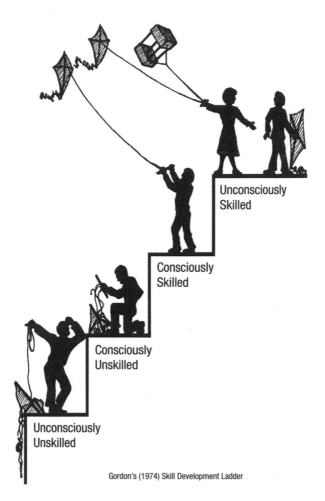

Unconsciously
Skilled

Consciously
Skilled

Consciously
Unskilled

Unconsciously
Unskilled

Gordon's (1974) Skill Development Ladder

© 1996 Performance Learning Systems, Inc.® from *Coaching Skills for Successful Teaching*®.

Figure 6.2

how to do this. This is an uncomfortable place to be when learning about anything.

The teacher can provide Jack with Encouraging Statements, focusing on the process. "Your efforts have started to pay off, Jack. Look how you have strung the kite to be ready to launch it."

Jack applies more effort to fly it and the kite falls flat on the ground. He has to rewind the kite string, but having done so before, his ability is now significantly increased by his effort, and in short order he has it back together ready to try again.

Here the teacher might give Evaluative Praise, focusing on the person. "I love how patient you are, Jack. You're going to get this up really soon, I can just tell."

Sure enough, Jack launches the kite and it's up, once, but then falls again. Jack is Consciously Skilled. He now knows what he is doing, but he can only do it if he concentrates, applies effort over and over, and keeps the focus.

At this juncture, the teacher can provide Feedback and Feedforward to further encourage Jack.

"Running down the hill was a good idea, Jack, and you did get the kite to fly." (Feedback—what he did in the past.) "Next time, why don't you try running a little bit faster and go all the way down the hill. I think the kite will go higher that way." (Feedforward—what he is to do in the future.)

Jack succeeds! He is flying the kite and yet is still very conscious of what he is doing. At this place, learners need the most encouragement and feedback/feedforward. This is the cheerleading spot that then moves them to the next rung of Gordon's Ladder, Unconsciously Skilled. Here not only can Jack fly his kite; he can fly two at once and mentor someone else, giving a friend encouragement to fly a kite at the same time.

At this rung, Jack is good at what he does. He has realized his vision, his belief. The success is all the more powerful here because he did go up the rungs of the ladder—his initial efforts paid off as his ability increased, he received the encouragement and feedback/feedforward he needed, and the goal is now sweeter because of it.

Encouragement comes in many forms and under many circumstances, and it always serves to shore up ability and ultimate success. Where would any of us be if someone hadn't encouraged us?

The following is a story about encouragement shared by Diane Moeller, principal of Kennedy Elementary School in St. Joseph, MN.

Several years into my teaching career, I had a young adult show up at my classroom door with the usual question: "Do you remember me?" She looked to be in her mid-twenties, so I started reviewing in my mind all of my classes of third graders from that era. There was something recognizable, but I could not put a name with this face.

As soon as she said her first name, Mary, I had an instant picture of this woman as the third grader I had encountered years earlier. I remembered the meek, shy little girl who had come to live with her elderly grandparents and thus came to our school mid-year due to being sexually abused by a family member. She only stayed for a few months and was again transferred. I remembered how withdrawn she was and that she often was rather disheveled looking. Her work and desk were similar.

I also remember that I taught this child with my heart. It seemed that the sloppy work was not as important as building her confidence. Other than this broad recollection of this student, I had no specific memories, but she did. She had come back to our small town to attend the funeral of her grandfather. So she stopped in to tell me that I had impacted her life more than anyone ever had.

Somewhat stunned, I stood there as Mary shared her life history since third grade. She had moved from foster home to foster home and eventually ended up on the streets in Minneapolis. She was on drugs and had become pregnant, but lost the baby in a miscarriage. Eventually, after treatment, she had gone back to high school and did graduate. Mary was now on her way to Texas to go to college. She showed me the letter of acceptance with pride. I remember thinking, "What a survivor!"

She went on to say, however, that this never would have happened if it weren't for her experience in my classroom. With my mouth agape, she recalled anecdote after anecdote that she remembered vividly. I wished I could say the same. The two that I remember her telling me are powerful testimonies to what sustains effort and what it can mean for struggling students.

One of her stories was about a program at our school that allowed students to work individually on a project during the month of February. The project was chosen from academics, arts or athletics. She chose to do a creative dance. The students could decide whether or not they wanted to showcase their project for the entire school.

Mary said that she did her dance for our class. She is sure now as an adult, that what she did was probably just a bunch of jumping around, but she said that I told her that I thought the entire school would love to see her dance. She said that she immediately refused, and that I was fine with that. But she went home and thought about it. She said she came the next day and told me she would do the dance. She said I responded with happiness and asked her how I could help her prepare. She said that I worked with her during one lunch period so that she would feel ready. She performed the dance for the entire school.

As this young woman reflected on this, she became tearful. She said, "I can still hear the school clapping for me. It was the only time in my life that anyone ever clapped for me." She said the memory of that sound is what got her through many tough times. She would remember that if she put forth some courage, she could do anything.

At this point I thought the conversation was over, but she went on. She asked me if I remembered the fire prevention poster contest. Of course I did because this was a tradition in our community. Each year during Fire Prevention Week, the students in the school would create safety posters. The firefighters would come in to judge each grade level and give out prizes.

Mary remembered that she had completed her poster and that I came by her desk, knelt down, and really studied it. She said that I asked her to tell me about it. As she did, she said I listened intently, like I really wanted to know about it. She said that as I got up, I looked at her and said that her idea was wonderful, but then asked her if she thought the firefighters would understand it if she could not tell them about it. (She said it was very sloppy and hard to read.)

Mary then recalled that after a few minutes she decided she would do the poster over and take her time to make it neat so that they would get the point. As she was telling me this, she reached into her purse. She pulled out a silver dollar, held it up and said, "I got first place!" She went on to tell me how many times she could have spent that dollar while living on the streets and needing to get some drugs, but she never did and vowed she never would. To her that silver dollar symbolized what she is capable of doing if she worked hard. She told me she held that dollar in her hand as she walked into the high school after drug rehabilitation to complete her education and graduate.

I wish I could remember these stories in the detail she did. I cannot. But I do know that her unexpected visit has stayed in my heart ever since. I am struck by the power of a teacher's daily interactions with students. I am struck that, for her, it took such little pieces of encouragement from me to motivate her to achieve. I am struck by the power of little successes to sustain a person through tough situations. I am also struck with the realization that compassion without enabling is a tough line to walk. How many other students have had barriers to learning? Have I been too compassionate and not able to move them forward?

I wish every teacher could be this lucky. We all have these stories, but I am fortunate to have had a student come back to tell me that what I said and did made a difference. Ironically, what she said to me has also made a difference in my life. I am probably much more attuned to my daily interactions than I was before.

Chapter 7:
Motivating Success

In our formula

$$\frac{\text{EFFORT} \times \textit{Ability} + \text{Manageable Task}}{\text{BELIEF} \quad \text{VISION}} = \textbf{SUCCESS!}$$

we know that applying effort causes one's ability to multiply. The ability increases with effort and an additional application of effort multiplies it further, all of which is applied to and impacts a manageable task. Shoring up the effort that multiplies ability when applied to a manageable task is a belief or vision of success. Belief engenders a sense of certainty that success will be achieved because it has been pictured in the mind's eye with strong emotion, and developed into a belief. That is a tremendously motivating engine.

But what drives *that* engine? What causes the effort in the first place? How do we keep the momentum going? Where do we get this motivation stuff?

In *Bringing Out the Best in People*, author Alan Loy McGinnis dispels the myth that no one really ever motivates anyone else, and that it all comes from within.[1] He contends that motivation does lurk within each of us and it often simply needs to be stimulated to come forth. We are all at our best when we have succeeded after being inspired or influenced by some person or event. Like effort, a little spark of motivation from an outside influence flames our own drive and the all-too-human desire to succeed. We are hardwired (genetically) to achieve and to succeed, as without that forward motion, we dwindle and die. It's a survival instinct.

I agree with McGinnis. Certainly the true drive of motivation comes from within. Yet I have seen countless incidents—and have experienced my own—that speak to the very powerful role of external motivation.

When developing my book *Wow! Adding Pizzazz to Teaching and Learning*, I discovered countless ingenious ways educators and administrators stimulated learning, motivated thinking, and otherwise added pizzazz and fun to learning, particularly when students began a new year or a new unit of study. WOWs are motivators. They arouse curiosity, stimulate an otherwise indifferent student, and soften the resistance to learning. Brain-based and fun, they create intrigue, a precursor to learning.

A WOW!

Here's one example —

A vocational education teacher enters the first day of class carrying an official looking leather briefcase complete with handle and locking hasps. He sets the briefcase flat on the desk and begins talking to the students. In a droning monotone, the teacher points out that this voc-ed program is very beneficial, but at times it may be boring. There will be lots of work to do, and it's going to be hard—awfully hard.

As the students' eyes begin to glaze over, their bodies shift and their feet shuffle uncomfortably. The teacher abruptly stops and asks in a loud voice, "Why are you here?!" Students look to one another surprised and a little shocked at his shift in tone, some perhaps wondering why, indeed, they *are* there.

Then the teacher snaps open the briefcase loudly. He tips it so students can see that it is full to the brim with neat stacks of money—$20 bills in many bundles, two layers deep. Each bundle is secured by a rubber band. The students gasp.

"Well," continues the teacher, now smiling and dropping the monotone, "You're here because this is the kind of money you can earn if you are qualified in this program." He slowly leafs through a bundle of money with his thumb, grinning out at the students who are now completely engaged and awestruck.

In creating his opening day "WOW," this teacher used one of the oldest gangster tricks in the world. He placed a $20 bill on the top and on the bottom of each bundle of cut up newspapers that served as unseen fillers. He also used one of the oldest motivators in the world: He intrigued his students to learn because the ultimate reward would be money.

Extrinsic rewards such as money and special favors or permissions serve as motivators, to be sure. Yet the strongest motivator to drive effort is the intrinsic motivator—the one that comes from within. This is the motivator that creates a desire to exert effort, increase ability, and *creates more of a challenge involving the manageability* of a task, all of which ultimately lead to success.

Multiplication Tables and a Banana Split

As an example, let's say a third-grade teacher wants to motivate her class to learn multiplication so that each one passes with flying colors. She hands out the books and goes over the multiplication concept. Then she assigns homework and says that as soon as everyone passes with a grade of C or above, each will get a banana split.

In every class, she goes over the assignment, the next table of multiplication, and reminds her students of the banana split that will come at the end. She may even have a picture of a banana split on the bulletin board.

While this serves as a motivation of sorts, for third graders this fuzzy image of a future banana split melts as weeks go by. They are pressured not only to learn, but also to pass with a grade of C or above and, until they all achieve that goal, the banana split remains elusive. They soon forget about the banana split and are not motivated. As the early television comedian and game show host Groucho Marx would say to participants who did not answer the question correctly, "Close, but no banana." These students may have started out motivated, but without continued envisioning of how effort leads to success, the vision of the banana split slowly fades.

Let's take the same example and look at what one teacher did not only to motivate with a banana split, but also to create an environment where the students themselves became intrinsically motivated and pulled together to achieve the envisioned result. It was "envisioned" because the teacher built on the vision of a completed goal—learning the concept and basic facts about multiplication—by reinforcing steps along the way, allowing for the effort to show increasing ability as students tackled each multiplication table, moving them inexorably toward the envisioned success.

Let's look at what happened in a real classroom.

When developing objectives for my third grade curriculum—to master the concept of multiplication and memorize the basic facts—I came across something that really added the motivating element for my students to put in the time and repetition needed to memorize facts. For each family of facts they mastered, they earned a part of a banana split. If they mastered their 2's they earned the bowl, if they passed their 3's they earned the ice cream, and so forth. Each day I asked them if they felt they were ready, and, if so, I would test them on the individual family of facts. If they weren't fluent, they worked harder. Nobody was going to get the banana split until everyone passed at least through the tens.

The beautiful element of this was not the banana split itself, but the community of learning that formed. It was not unusual for kids to be quizzing each other. Mornings before school became a time when kids would ask other kids to help them make their next set of flash cards. At the end of the day, one could hear them asking each other if they had their flash cards to take home to study. There was not a sense of competition at all. We were all in this together. It did not seem to matter that some students passed right away and others needed more time. It did not matter that some needed to use manipulatives to see the picture. We played lots of flash card games as a full class, but not to see whom would win. We competed against ourselves as a whole unit. Did we get through the set of flash cards in less time than the day before?

It took about two months, but everyone finally did pass. The celebration was huge. The ice cream was the sweetest these kids had ever tasted because it was the fruit of their hard work.

What was my role in this group success? It really was to re-move any barriers to learning, to provide assistance in a variety of ways, and to keep them motivated. I soon realized that to sustain their effort for this lengthy process, I needed far more than the banana split. I needed an *esprit de corps* that can only happen with intrinsic motivation. Each day we celebrated hard work. I asked students the kinds of questions that had them thinking about how good it felt to work this hard. Of course, I enlisted the help of parents to do the same at home. They, too, were amazed that these third graders were so pumped to learn these facts.

I learned a great deal from these banana splits. I found out that kids will work hard when we ask them to invest themselves and make some choices. I did not tell them when they had to have these facts learned—they decided that. I did not tell them what set to work on each night; they were self-directed to take care of that. This was not an exceptional group of kids. It was the average sort of group with some high achievers, some strugglers, some special education students, and so on. But they all achieved success.

That success, of course, was also varied by my teacher

discretion. Was it okay that some students needed to complete the quiz by memory, but that as I quizzed others, I allowed some mental calculation? Of course. That is the beauty of differentiated instruction. And they all got to the same goal: they knew that they could deal with these pesky multiplication facts. They all experienced a degree of success due to their own hard work that led them to believe that multiplication facts were possible for them.[2]

A Question of Beliefs

Again, the underlying need for a motivated learner encompasses a belief that he or she can succeed. When I stress this point to educators in presentations, I often receive the query, "Well, Steve, I understand the need for a student to believe in him- or herself, to envision success. But how do you get a student to realize his or her beliefs? What if they say they don't really have any beliefs?"

Sadly, this is often the case, and particularly at the middle and high school levels where students' belief in themselves and their ability to achieve success are often muddled by hormones and peer pressure that have them self-consciously taking a hard look at themselves at every pass. Alan Loy McGinnis, mentioned above, is a family therapist whose patients appeared similarly confused about their belief system. He suggests in his book *Bringing Out the Best in People* that anyone feeling he or she is bereft of beliefs should make a list of at least 20 things of which he or she is certain. It does not matter what comes up—"I have trouble waking up"; "My dog hates letter carriers";

---

[2] Used with permission of Diane Moeller, Principal, Kennedy Elementary School, St. Joseph, MN.

"School sucks"; "I'm going to college." What matters is that the belief encompasses something certain for that person.[3]

From that McGinnis points out that the person did, indeed, have beliefs and that the person created those beliefs. Beliefs come from thoughts and emotions, so a belief that says, "I don't really have any beliefs" (with despair and resignation as an undertone) can be off-set by an opposing belief: "I believe strongly in a lot of things" (with hope and enthusiasm and certainty underscoring the statement). It's important to point out to students that they are the ones deciding on their thoughts and their beliefs. It's a choice—a really simple choice. Choose to believe they can't succeed or choose to believe they can. It's up to them.

A report titled, "The Silent Epidemic," by John M. Bridgeland, John J. Dilulio, Jr., and Karen Burke Morison looks at the alarming level of high school dropouts. The report, funded through Civic Enterprises in association with Peter D. Hart Research Associates for the Bill & Melinda Gates Foundation, cites many reasons for this trend, allowing there is no single reason that overreaches all others. Nearly half (47 percent) indicated classes were not interesting. Students were bored and disengaged. Sixtynine percent said they "were not motivated or inspired to work hard, 80 percent did one hour or less of homework each day in high school, two-thirds would have worked harder if more was demanded of them (higher academic standards and more studying

---

and homework), and 70 percent were confident they could have graduated if they had tried."

Focusing on Life Skills

One of the recommendations in the report to help students stay in school pointed to strengthening the connection between school and work. "Four out of five (81 percent) said there should be more opportunities for real-world learning and some in the focus groups called for more experiential learning. They said students needed to see the connection between school and getting a good job."

A graduate course developed by Performance Learning Systems, Inc. called *Teaching the Skills of the 21st Century®* covers teaching life skills students can use in the workplace for jobs that may not even have been invented yet. This course looks at school and teaching in a variety of alternative ways given the technology and fast-paced world of today. It suggests teachers make a paradigm shift from teaching content, school subjects or disciplines alone, to teaching the content along with the process or life skills that are being implemented as the student applies learning. An awareness of these process skills *as* the student is learning the subject matter instills the value of using those skills in any subject. These important process skills translate into life skills used in the workplace and beyond. Knowing that a student is analyzing, summarizing, interviewing, presenting, questioning, listening, or otherwise employing life skills as he or she is doing them sinks that process skill into permanent memory.

Figure 7.1 shows traditional teaching to content with little connection to life subjects.

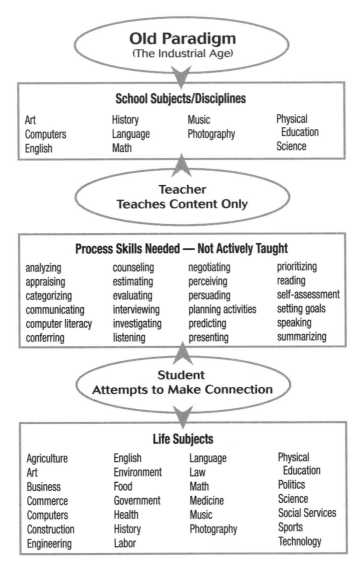

Figure 7.1

Figure 7.2 graphically depicts how teaching process skills along with content motivates students because these skills can be applied to employment opportunities.

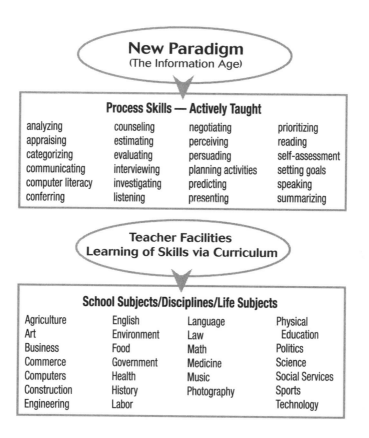

New Paradigm
(The Information Age)

Process Skills — Actively Taught

analyzing	counseling	negotiating	prioritizing
appraising	estimating	perceiving	reading
categorizing	evaluating	persuading	self-assessment
communicating	interviewing	planning activities	setting goals
computer literacy	investigating	predicting	speaking
conferring	listening	presenting	summarizing

Teacher Facilities
Learning of Skills via Curriculum

School Subjects/Disciplines/Life Subjects

Agriculture	English	Language	Physical
Art	Environment	Law	Education
Business	Food	Math	Politics
Commerce	Government	Medicine	Science
Computers	Health	Music	Social Services
Construction	History	Photography	Sports
Engineering	Labor		Technology

Figure 7.2

Applying process skills to potential jobs is particularly useful for students who may not attend college but who, nevertheless, need to understand and effectively use process skills to be successfully employed. They need to make a continued effort to learn to be able to compete in the workplace, whether they have the opportunity to attend college or not. A recent issue of *Education Week* cites a study by the National Center for High Education Management Systems that speaks to the large disparity between wages of those employees who attended higher education and those who did not. Yet given this disparity, students are more and more bypassing college for the workplace, despite risking an apparent loss in salary. Citing the study, *Education Week* states, "for every 100 students who start high school, only 67 earn a diploma within four years. Of those, only 38 enter college, 26 are still enrolled after their sophomore year, and just 18 graduate on time with either an associates' or a bachelor's degree."

Clearly, continued effort on the part of students can offset what appears to be a downward spiral among those who may graduate from high school, but still fall out of post-secondary training and education. In many cases they cannot keep up; in others, the job market has more immediate appeal and meaning, even though the high school graduate with post-secondary training continues to garner more salary than one who does not continue into advanced learning.

These statistics may be interesting to students who, for whatever economic, social, or value-based reasons, are not college bound. They can be motivated by the fact that, regardless of whether one goes to college or not—and there are now increasingly other alternatives—learning how to compete for jobs with high-level skills is crucial to surmount the widening gap between low-paying and higher-level jobs.

A high school student given the assignment of interviewing someone in the community about an open space initiative in the city, one that would preserve wetlands, for example, discovers the social, political, environmental, and economic issues facing the community. Yet he or she also learns the key skills of interviewing, listening, paraphrasing, asking open-ended questions, conferring, hypothesizing, investigating, summarizing, and presenting—skills that are crucial for landing a job and keeping it.

The key here—one we will cover more fully in Chapter 9—is to let the student in on the point of doing an interview. Let him or her know that, yes, the assignment is to learn the many issues surrounding the open space initiative; perhaps to select and delve into any one of these issues to learn more about the socioeconomic, political, or environmental impacts, but also just as importantly to learn the skills he or she will need to be successful in life. Becoming skilled in areas such as communication, presentation, problem solving, decision making, and anticipating not only makes good fodder for employment opportunities, it maintains success as a citizen, a voter, a spouse, a parent, and a successful member of the human race. The more we can point to the learning as we teach it, the more relevant and meaningful it is to the student. Giving him or her the big picture—"you're doing this because"— lends the student not only respect and trust, but provides the motivation to do it for him- or herself, not simply to satisfy the teacher.

The Motivation of Feedback

Feedback, a crucial brain-based teaching technique, also happens to be a strong motivator. As students apply effort, immediate and frequent feedback allows them to measure their increased ability and motivates them to continue. In Richard Sagor's *Motivating Students and Teachers in an Era of Standards,* he tells a great story about the need for students to receive feedback in order to maintain an effort.[4] He declares he never understood why students went out for track and field in Oregon when it typically rains every afternoon. Though it was three hours of cold rain and soggy turf, they suited up every day, went out onto the field, and ran through the drills.

Finally he realized it was the tape measure and stopwatch used every day to measure progress that provided them with immediate feedback and motivated them to continue their effort and hard work. They were motivated to improve their speed, increase the length of their jumps. The numerical feedback from the tape measure and stopwatch, coupled with the observation and encouragement from the coach, gave them the information they needed to be motivated to continue to improve.

I've heard golfers profess it never rains on a golf course (and, of course, it does) implying that while they are keeping their scores and working every shot to stay at or below par, the effort of doing that—and the feedback reflected in the number of strokes played (or not played) for each hole—mitigates the fact that it is pouring down rain. They simply don't notice!

Celebrate the Effort

The more we can do to instill in students the importance and significance of effort, the better off they will be as they travel into the world of work and life. Give immediate and frequent feedback. Provide feedforward. Celebrate the achievement of effort. Celebrations signal success and reinforce a student's belief in himself or herself. Too often we pass by the final achievement without acknowledging the effort that went into it. And the effort was cumulative. That last effort did not cause the success; a succession of efforts created the success, just as one degree of heat pushes the 211-degree water to 212 and boiling, but that degree of heat needed 210 degrees ahead of it to reach boiling point.

It's important to build celebration into our lives because it is celebration that builds perseverance. Celebrate the results of the efforts, and effort plus perseverance results in success that warrants a celebration.

A student's belief—his or her dreams—are a precursor to celebrations. Dreams drive effort. Celebrate both the dream and the effort; they are a powerful pair.

In Chapter 6 we relayed educator and author Alfie Kohn's point about avoiding the use of workplace metaphors when talking to students about learning—they are in school to learn, not to "work."[5] On the other hand, the workplace of today has more and more become a learning organization. A student who grasps that a real-life assignment, such as an interview that requires research, thoroughness, effort, and the very important process skills that will be useful throughout his or her life, begins to understand the meld of learning and working. The learning effort he or she applies to a live "real-world" application begins to make sense as he or she realizes this effort is a model for the workplace.

The value of learning and applying effort to a task that has meaning begins to look a whole lot like being a productive employee, using effort and skills to increase ability and achieve success. And in the workplace, success goes well beyond the reward of a banana split. It translates into a livelihood, and also into satisfaction, the key reason people put in productive days at work. Making the learn/work connection to students in high school, and even well before that, serves as motivation for them to apply effort to manageable and, particularly, meaningful tasks.

[5] From "Students Don't Work—They Learn by Alfie Kohn as first appeared in *Education Week* on September 3, 1997. Reprinted with permission from the author.

Wherever and however possible, we as educators need to create opportunities to uncover students' beliefs and values so that the tasks we do ask them to complete are meaningful as well as manageable. Generating an environment that elicits the inner motivation students need to succeed may seem daunting, particularly given budget constraints, classrooms that are less than desirable, and class sizes preventing the intimacy desired when talking to students about their values and their beliefs. Yet with a little imagination and effort a classroom can become its own learning organization with elements of brain-compatibility that engender learning that is relevant, useful, necessary, motivating, and fun.

In the next chapter, we'll look at how classrooms can be transformed into learning laboratories and how bringing real-world applications to learning naturally piques motivation.

Chapter 8:
Tapping Excitement

Make it Brain Based

Walking in, you can't help but notice the elementary classroom sports several aquariums and an earthworm farm, and you definitely notice the box turtle roaming free. A ball python and a red rat snake reside in their glass-enclosed home, and young leopard geckos live right next door in a similar container.

A mini-museum of clear boxes houses snake skins, fossils, and rocks; other examples of nature's detritus line a shelf that encompasses the room. Two canaries sing brightly, and a tall aviary houses four families of finches who click and coo to one another. Two rabbits hop around the garden outside the classroom. Music plays softly from a CD player.

Across town at the local high school, you enter a classroom housing many comfy looking couches, plants, easy chairs, and bookshelves. Some students loll on the couches, books in hand. A circle of chairs occupies the center of the room, where several students face one another in animated discussion. The walls are covered with colorful posters depicting various places around the world. Some convey up beat messages. A fish tank sits on a wide table near a window. Bubbles from the pump glisten in the sunshine, as tropical fish glide softly through them.

If these seem like creative, exciting places for learning, they are. They are brain-compatible classrooms, each containing the peripheral stimuli, color, music, nature, an open atmosphere conducive to exploration and fun; a safe environment for learning.

We now know enough about brain research and learning to create a classroom that reflects how the brain learns best, and with minimal cost or exertion. Sure, some classrooms today are pathetically dilapidated, in disrepair, with environments resembling incarceration rather than education. It's a national shame. Yet even these classrooms can be brightened and made more stimulating.

A crack in the wall? Cover it with a poster. No windows? Have a painting party and create a beautiful scene out a make-believe window. If nothing else, bring in music, plants, balloons—anything colorful and stimulating. The brain responds to color and sensory richness. Mobiles and toys that make noise or feel good to the touch stimulate infants. This doesn't change as we grow older. The brain lives in Technicolor and responds to sound, light, smell, taste, and feeling. Eliminate wherever possible the bland, the boring, the black-and-white, linear, and ugly from your classroom. You will be amazed at the acceleration of student effort and student learning in an environment that supports it.

In Chapter 5 we took a peek at learning styles, an extremely important brain-based component of teaching which suggested we address all students' learning styles, whether sensory, organizational, or temperament types. Beyond that, brain-based teaching and learning has been well documented and implemented in schools throughout the country. In *Exceeding Expectations: A User's Guide to Implementing Brain Research in the Classroom.* (once titled *ITT: The Model Integrated Thematic Instruction*), Susan Kovalik and Karen Olsen identify and describe eight elements that, when present in teaching and learning, cause the brain to be both prepared and stimulated to make productive effort.[1] Kovalik describes these elements as:

Absence of Threat
Meaningful Content
Choices
Adequate Time
Enriched Environment
Collaboration
Immediate Feedback
Mastery (Application)

---

[1] From Susan J. Kovalik and Karen D. Olsen, *Exceeding Expectations: A User's Guide to Implementing Brain Research in the Classroom, 3rd Edition.* Copyright © 2006 Susan J. Kovalik; distributed by Books for Educators, Inc.

When applying Kovalik's elements to our own formula of

$$\frac{\text{EFFORT} \times \textit{Ability} + \text{Manageable Task}}{\text{BELIEF} \quad \text{VISION}} = \textbf{SUCCESS!}$$

we can see the importance of ensuring students that their belief and vision are supported by both the teacher and fellow students.

As mentioned in Chapter 2, Richard Sagor recommends in *Motivating Students and Teachers in an Era of Standards* that students essentially buy in to another's goals, even going so far as to have each student complete a "Goal Affirmation Sheet" and develop a plan of action, plotting out a viable strategy for the achievement of his or her personal goals.[2] This is not dissimilar to what managers and employees require in the workplace, and Sagor even refers to the "Academic Coach" and the "Knowledge Worker" when describing his prescribed involvement of student, parent, and teacher/coach in a student's vision.

Once this action plan is completed, Sagor suggests a review of the results in a report provided by the "knowledge worker" that responds to these questions:

1. *What was my goal?*
2. *What did I believe I needed to do to achieve my goal?*
3. *What did I do?*
4. *What were the results?*

---

[2] From *Motivating Students and Teachers in an Era of Standards* by Richard Sagor. Copyright © 2003 by Association for Supervision and Curriculum Development. Reprinted by Permission. The Association for Supervision and Curriculum Development is a worldwide community of educators advocating sound policies and sharing best practices to achieve the success of each learner. To learn more, visit ASCD at www.ascd.org.

While the action plan provides accountability, it also most certainly represents the elements of brain-based learning as suggested by Kovalik. With a student's belief in his or her success shored up by support from fellow students, parents, and teacher/coach, the student is certain to be reassured his or her belief in success is attainable. There is a clear **Absence of Threat**.

The student's effort toward success as well as the goal he or she has chosen delivers **Meaningful Content** to the student and to others. He or she has **Choices** about the vision and the plan of action. There is **Adequate Time** as it is the student who develops his or her Goal Affirmation Sheet with prescribed tasks to accomplish—efforts to expend—to achieve results. The support of others in the process provides an **Enriched Environment, Collaboration,** and **Immediate Feedback.** Finally, as the student achieves his or her results—the success driven by shared belief and vision—there is **Mastery**.

The knowledge we have about how the brain takes in, stores, organizes, and communicates information can help us motivate student effort. A brain-compatible environment that includes music, color, and peripheral stimuli creates opportunities for what Eric Jensen refers to, in *Completing the Puzzle: The brain-compatible approach to learning*, as "state changes."[3] These signal to the brain—and the student who resides beneath it—that something new is about to occur. The brain perks up at the beginning of a new or intriguing situation. It recalls where it is when

[3] From Eric Jensen, *Completing the Puzzle: The Brain-Compatible Approach to Learning*, pp. 38-39, Copyright © 1997 by Corwin Press. Reprinted by permission of Corwin Press.

new learning occurs. That is why you can have a thought to go and get a book in another room, arrive at the room, and completely forget why you are there. It is only when you return to where you were when you had that first thought that you say, "Oh, yes. The book!"

State changes mean mood changes, environmental changes. Dimming the lights, adding music, or moving to a different whiteboard all create state change. It can mean literally moving students to a new location or having them stand and stretch or otherwise move their bodies. Motion changes emotion and thus the brain responds favorably. Creating an experience for the student that intrigues, creates curiosity, anticipation, and fun—what I've called a "WOW"— triggers a state change and motivates the brain to learn.

What we know about the brain is that it is hard-wired to learn. Without stimulation, dendrites and neurons in the brain stop growing. The brain dies. Learning is like food to the brain; it must have it to survive.

In *Making Connections: Teaching and the Human Brain*, Renate Nummela and Geoffrey Caine define brain-based learning this way:[4]

> *"In many ways, the brain is like the heart or lungs. Each organ has a natural function. The brain learns because that is its job. Moreover, the brain has a virtually inexhaustible capacity to learn. Each healthy human brain, irrespective of a person's age, sex,*

nationality, or cultural background, comes equipped with a set of exceptional features:

- *The ability to detect patterns and to make approximations*
- *Phenomenal capacity for various types of memory*
- *The ability to self-correct and learn from experience by way of analysis of external data and self-reflection, and*
- *An inexhaustible capacity to create.*

If everyone has these capacities, why are we struggling in our ability to educate?"

Why, indeed?

Live-Event Learning®

In "real life," we are learning all the time, even when unaware of it. New problems, new technology, new information, new people, and new skills—all require learning; all require effort. There are often real consequences if the information is *not* learned, the effort *not* expended.

To motivate students to apply effort and achieve success, we often only need to look at life itself. Any true experiential learning experience includes aspects of life that not only stimulate effort; they require it. Most schools are still operating in a culture where the teacher delivers and the student learns. The teacher provides; the student takes. The teacher offers knowledge; the student tries and/or succeeds in understanding it. Educators deliver the information, the knowledge, and the skills in what we call lesson plans or units of learning. This continuum, Figure 8.1, demonstrates some of the methods teachers use to deliver the learning.

Textbook/ Manipulation	Simulation	Real Life Live Event

Figure 8.1

On the left is the traditional textbook learning and manipulations. I jokingly refer to manipulations as any trick, gimmick, or strategy a teacher is not too proud to use and still call him or herself a teacher! Whatever works, right?

Manipulations can be simple strategies, such as putting information the students need to remember into a rap. Students sing through the list of United States presidents or the 50 states or recite prepositions in ways they can recall them.

I met a teacher who taught students where to place commas in sentences by having them come to the front of the room and stomp one foot each time a comma was appropriately called for in the sentences she read. When the students returned to their seats to quietly complete a lesson, you could see an orchestra of spasmodically stamping feet, as each student stepped up to the task of inserting proper commas.

But where in that manipulation is a desire for a student to exert effort? Is there a vision or belief attached to the learning that the student believes in and thus drives the effort? Is the student's task a manageable one ensuring his or her success?

In the middle of the continuum are activities that simulate real life, such as role-plays, games, mock trials, etc. In Paducah, KY, fifth graders at Farley Elementary School participated in the "Take Stock in Kentucky" program sponsored by the Kentucky Council on Economic Education. Based on the national "Stock Market Game," these students were among 1,600 in Kentucky who researched companies and invested $100,000 in imaginary money over the course of 10 weeks. The students' results were based on actual market performance of stocks.

This simulation—an activity that mimics real life without the real consequences—nevertheless allows more access to learning that resembles the right side of the continuum—learning through real live events. While students learn monetary values and the vagaries of the stock market in an exciting, competitive manner, they also remain distant, and the consequences of winning or losing money are not real. The learning can remain static and fixed with specific predetermined outcomes—for example, what we as educators want them to learn—and the students' individual experience can become diluted. Since simulations are contrived, the student can either passively receive the information or get into it, and the outcome of the activity remains the same.

Leslie Hart's seminal book *Human Brain and Human Learning—Updated* quotes an insight from M. C. Wittrock, a professor of educational psychology in the Graduate School of Education at the University of California, Los Angeles. Wittrock claims:[5]

"The brain does not usually learn in the sense of accepting or recording information from teachers. The brain is not a passive consumer of information. Instead, it actively constructs its own interpretations of information and draws inferences from it. The brain ignores some information and selectively attends to other information.

In short, a teacher aggressively instructing a class of 25 is actually not addressing a group at all, but rather 25 individual brains, each of whom will attend to what it chooses, then process that input in an individual way, relating it (if at all) only to previous individual input or experience."

What Wittrock refers to is not only the individuality of each student's learning style, his or her brain, but also underscores our discussion about the need to provide differentiated instruction. While this may seem daunting to educators already strapped with more than most can handle, to the rescue comes the right side of the Figure 8.1 continuum. The far right involves real life and uses teaching techniques called "live events." These are lessons percolated up through real time. They can be unstructured and the learning can vary from student to student. Thus they provide a richness of learning that motivates students who can also individualize their learning. Doing so allows teachers to focus on the learning he or she believes and envisions for the students, and ultimately results in less work on the part of the teacher as "life itself" provides the valuable lesson. The teacher observes from the sidelines, guiding learning to what he or she intended and then debriefing the learning to "help it sink in."

A course, *Discovering the Power of Live-Event Learning®,* offered by Performance Learning Systems, provides in-depth understanding and practice in weaving live events, real life experiences, into curriculum and instruction whenever possible.

The instructional tools spectrum in Figure 8.2 shows various methods of delivering instruction, and where each type falls in terms of its motivation and stimulation to engage students and engender student effort.

Live-Event Learning
Instructional Methods

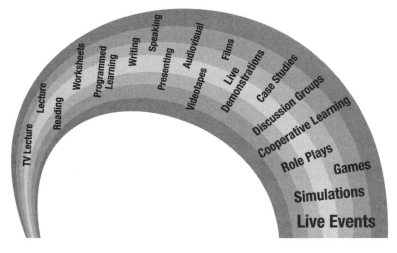

© 1996 Performance Learning Systems, Inc. ®

Figure 8.2

Live events, on the right, are the most enriched; televised lecture, on the left, the least captivating.

More elaborate live events include interacting in a real-world environment, as we will see from the examples below. First let's look at what constitutes a "live event." It is above all a learning experience for students. The teacher's role is to provide the opportunity for the live event to take place, to guide the event as it unfolds and, most importantly, to debrief that learning occurred in the process.

A live event is brain-based. It contains all the elements that trigger the brain to come alive and exert effort, use skills and apply knowledge, and it has the built-in capacity to engender motivation because there are real things happening in real time. The student's individual experience and imprint on the live event is consequential, real.

Live Events have **relevance**. Students realize there is a need to learn in order to take part in the event. There is often an emotion and the brain recalls prior similar experiences and their outcomes.

Live Events are **multisensory,** engaging all the senses. Learning styles jump into gear, as live events by their nature cover the spectrum of visual, auditory, kinesthetic, and tactual senses.

Live Events take place in a **real environment**. Rather than reading about or doing mock activities that exemplify pH balance in water, the elementary student is actually changing water in a goldfish bowl and measuring the pH. Instead of creating a mock trial, middle or high school students actually visit a legal proceeding at the courthouse. Alternatively, rather than reenact the legislative process in a mock House of Representatives, students can together create, support, or otherwise work toward getting a specific piece of real legislation passed.

Live Events involve **emotions**. The brain recalls information when there is emotion attached. Shifting emotions shifts perspective; shifting perspective offers an opportunity to shift learning. Students excited about a project or afraid of it or worried about it or frustrated by it are nevertheless engaged in the learning of it.

Live Events involve process skills similar to those we looked at in Chapter 7—ones that combine the content of learning with the life skills associated with that learning. These are basic skills used in everyday life: analyzing, summarizing, anticipating, implying, predicting, listening, communicating, negotiating, and persevering.

Finally Live Events have **real consequences**. This element seems to be the most difficult to create in schools, even in Live-Event Learning situations. Students have to see a real consequence attached to the learning involved in the live event in order to be motivated to exert the required effort. If they don't pull off the fund raiser, there are many consequences.

Since schools, by their very structure, exist in a vacuum separate from the world "outside," the consequences may not always appear to be there. If the experiment fails in school, students may simply leave it and go outside, where they are not aware of experiments they undertake on a daily basis as no teacher stands by to point out the learning. In those "experiments," the consequences are real. Bringing that concept of responsibility and accountability for student effort in real life back into the classroom bridges the unnatural gap that exists between school and "real life."

The more real and alive the lesson, the more students will see the consequences of *not* succeeding. Perhaps here more than ever, the student needs to understand his or her vision or belief and the consequence to him or her should that vision or belief not be attained. That's a consequence that, if not understood, can translate into downshifting and a sense of failure that can haunt the student for the rest of his or her life.

Real consequences mean something is at stake; it counts. Going back to the fund raiser, they may fail to raise money. Dropping the fish on the floor when changing the tank water means the fish dies. Not understanding what happened in the courthouse or governing bodies may or may not have real consequences. Much of that depends on how the teacher frames the purpose of the learning. And "purpose" provides the underpinning for consequence. What is the student's purpose in learning it? What happens if he or she doesn't?

This goes back to success. If a student has as a goal to learn how government works—or perhaps simply how a bill he or she was studying makes its way through the system—and then attends a legislative session, the consequence is almost naturally amped up. After all, it is the student's vision—he or she has ownership of it—and here is a real-life, real-time, multisensory, relevant, and emotional experience for the student to have the vision realized. The consequences of not learning what the student came to learn are more internal than external. It was merely a waste of time.

In my experience of watching students engaged in Live-Event Learning, I can say I have never known a student or a teacher to conclude the live event was ever a waste of time. In the Foreword to this book, Joe

Hasenstab mentions how senior projects, mostly all live events, were never seen by the students as a waste of time. There is *always* learning. To me, the real consequence of wasted time becomes far more prevalent in units of learning bereft of any aliveness for the student—or the teacher for that matter.

Students in Nat Williams Elementary K-6 magnet school in Lubbock, TX created two "towns" within the school. Each had its own post office, its own ZIP code. Each student and adult had his or her own address, and all were listed in the school directory. Students sorted and delivered mail and assisted their postal patrons at the counter. A student postmaster oversaw the activities. Pressure increased when holidays occurred, and students delivering the mail had to keep on top of demand. It's part of an authentic learning program at the school, and at each step, students were made aware of the learning: reading, writing, sorting, time management, customer service, accountability, responsibility, government, public relations.

At Ballard West Elementary School in Slater, Iowa, first graders launched and now run their own business enterprise. They opened a bakery within the school. First they interviewed bakers in the community to learn what they needed. They created a name and an in-school advertising campaign for their bakery through flyers and jingles broadcast over the school's PA system. Students made the baked goods or contracted with parent suppliers. They sold the goods at set times two days a week, enlisting the support of parents and teachers. In the process they learned about writing and creating graphics for flyers; they studied math while determining interest on their initial loan, cost of baked goods, negotiating purchase price with parent suppliers; they handled money and determined profit or loss. And the list goes on.

Planting a garden, raising money for the school band, balancing a real checkbook, creating greeting cards to sell as a fundraiser to save the rain forest, selling school T-shirts to pay for a field trip, ordering supplies over the Internet, planning and carrying out a field trip, and redesigning the classroom—whatever project, process, or cause that ties learning into a live event generates the enthusiasm and excitement that accompanies all true learning.

With live events, students feel compelled to exert effort. The effort pays off. There is the real thing in front of them. If one try doesn't do it, they exhibit choice and drive to try again, increase their abilities until they get it, manage it, finish it, and deliver it.

The Millennial Generation, born 1982 to 2005, tend to have values inherited from either Boomer parents or grandparents—or perhaps we have all come to an age when saving the planet or involving ourselves in causes has become a primary need. Technology has brought the world's problems vividly to our living rooms, and no one knows that better than the Millennial student. They have had the world in the palm of their hands since birth. What they have seen has made them realistic, and it has also created in them the desire to do more than succeed on the corporate ladder (only to be torn down by scandals) or to sit by as the planet and its people suffer.

After September 11, 2001 and its disaster, these students have rallied to offer services while absorbing remarkable skills and knowledge in the process. Here are a few examples of high school students fully engaged in Live-Event Learning from What Kids Can Do, Inc., Voices and Work From the Next Generation, Next Generation Press.

In Mukilteo, WA, students at Harbour Pointe Middle School are hoping to persuade their school board to use an alternative fuel in their school buses. Students watched an instructor from a University of Washington environmental program blend a concoction of vegetable oil, methanol, and lye to create biodiesel, a less-polluting alternative fuel. They researched and studied its potential for months. Ultimately, they presented their case to the Mukilteo School Board in April 2006. They were the youngest participants at a biodiesel conference in Seattle where they presented their project.

In Newark Valley, NY, upstate teenagers traveled to the shareholder meeting of Altria Group, parent company of Philip Morris in East Hanover, NJ to protest Marlboro cigarettes, 50 years after the brand was introduced to international markets.

Eleven students at George Jenkins High School in Lakeland, Florida are participating in a $1 million study of the Caribbean fruit fly—the "Caribfly"—to answer questions about how it breeds and how far and quickly it spreads. Its aim is to develop computer models to predict future outbreaks that wreak havoc on agriculture in the area.

The prospects of Global Warming is sparking real life projects in schools across the nation.

Beyond creating the motivation to exert effort to learn and succeed, beyond shoring up a student's vision and belief in his or her success and in him- or herself, enriched lessons and live-event learning empower students. Students take ownership of their own learning and experience a sense of power and freedom that can carry them throughout their lives. And, as we shall see in the next chapter, adding empowerment to effort, motivation, belief, and success also inspires teachers and administrators to become rejuvenated in their professions and their own learning.

Chapter 9: Empowering Achievement

In Chapter 1 we looked at what constitutes effort—that exertion, that repeated attempt to increase ability, and therefore success. It often involved something new, a challenge, and may have put us out of our comfort zone. It even created discomfort. Those who exert effort simply to get out of bed or speak a full sentence or take a step with a new prosthesis—and the list goes on—nevertheless continue the effort because of an innate drive to succeed.

Effort is the kernel from which success grows. The kernel becomes cultivated with an engendering belief and a vision of success. As effort increases, ability increases exponentially, particularly as manageable tasks combine with both external and intrinsic influences. Real consequences and real experiences reflect immediate feedback on the results of efforts expended.

Good Ole Hard Work

Embedded within the effort that leads to success is the simple notion of hard work. Mark Thompson, director of the National Educator Program, Tampa, FL, asks teacher participants in his classes to recall something they did for extra credit as a student that, to this day, they're particularly proud of.

Most participants instantly recall a project that highlighted what they could do and who they were. When pulling common characteristics from teachers in the class, they consistently cite that the project occurred in the real world, outside of the classroom. It was not abstract and benign. It had real impact. And all remember that it was hard work. They remember there was a risk of failure in the project (consequences), and it required them to work on it a long time, not just throw it together.

So often we hesitate to give students hard work for fear they will not be actively engaged in school; it may knock them out. Yet often it is just the opposite. Given an opportunity and an incentive, students jump into hard work, particularly if it exists in real-time, real-world environments.

If it's a large project, putting students in teams and dividing out the work to be done according to strengths not only provides teamwork and accountability, it brings in an element of unpredictability. The team members are in this together, and the outcome is uncertain. They may ultimately come up with information they can teach others in the classroom—even information new to the teacher, and that provides a real enticement to work even harder, because knowing something the teacher may not know represents its own success.

The element of uncertainty exudes excitement, many examples of which are described in my book *WOW! Adding Pizzazz to Teaching and Learning.* This combination of uncertainty and excitement serves as the foundation for Odyssey of the Mind, an international educational program that provides creative problem-solving opportunities for students from kindergarten through college. Projects extend beyond the school day and focus on problem solving. Students apply creativity to solve problems that range from building mechanical devices to presenting their own interpretation of literary classics. They then bring their solutions to competition on the local, state, and global level. Thousands of teams from throughout the U.S. and about 25 other countries participate in the program.

The Power of Empowerment

In contrast, tackling a project on their own provides the final and possibly the most powerful element to tap student effort: empowerment. Students taking charge of their own learning take ownership of the outcome, whether ownership of a vision or the fulfillment of a goal or the accomplishment of a task. Allowing the learning to occur because the student is driving it beats any state mandate for learning I have ever come across.

Live events lend themselves to empowerment, because the teacher cannot orchestrate the outcome. The student takes control as he or she goes through the event and, yes, the teacher debriefs the learning embedded within the experience by asking the student to note where he or she may have applied math, for example, or how and where prioritizing might have occurred, or what science he or she learned. And perhaps the teacher had that set up ahead of time, knowing the live event might cover content areas that he or she could then debrief.

But my take is that, if a student is capable of undertaking a project or a real-life experience and handling whatever it is successfully, then wouldn't that student also know, to a certain extent, what he or she learned? What would be the harm in asking what he or she learned, even if it did not match the prescribed learning formulated by the teacher ahead of time? Certainly many classroom teachers are pleasantly surprised—and maybe embarrassed—when students point out something they learned that wasn't in the ole rubric.

Likewise, job-embedded learning for teachers involves teachers trying a new approach, an experiment, perhaps a live event for the first time, and when they have coaches the coach observes and debriefs with them afterward. While the coach may assume the teacher learned x, y, and z, the teacher may have had insights a, b, c, and an increase in awareness not detectable by the coach, but nevertheless a learning for him or her.

Real learning, at its best, is messy. It is not laid out in linear fashion, and uniformly gobbled up by students of whatever age or profession. The world of work is a learning environment, and learning is often chaotic, experimental, fraught with trials and errors. And in the world of work, as in the classroom, employees who are empowered to take on projects on their own, who are given numerous opportunities for feedback and receive plenty of feedforward tend to become excited about what they do. They bring passion and added effort to the equation.

Teachers at the beginning of a school year often develop their lesson plans and units of study and feel empowered and excited about them. "I'm going to teach English Lit this year in a way I've never done it before, and I'm so excited about it."

But then they go into the classroom, and students, since they have not been involved in the planning, do not share the excitement. They don't know what they are going to do next, so they wait to be "fed" the teaching without a lot of enthusiasm. There's a dearth of "WOW" surrounding the incoming class.

Students at the beginning of learning are like Jack on the first rung of Gordon's Ladder described in Chapter 6. They don't know what they don't know; they are unconsciously unskilled. Only when they become consciously unskilled does effort occur. Giving students the big picture (a brain-based element) of what the teacher has in mind for the year, spoken with the enthusiasm he or she feels—coupled with asking students for their input on what else they might want to learn and how—can result in an immediately empowered classroom ready to tackle the year.

Granted, the level to which a teacher can get input from students will be age- and grade-dependent, but even introducing choices (yet another brain-based component) not only might provide a sense of ownership over the learning, it also reveals preferred learning styles. Asking fourth graders if they want to write a story together or put on a play or read to one another in order to learn about frogs requires a flexible teacher who can even change direction or plans made. But if the outcome is a motivated learner exerting effort and achieving success, then that's an opportunity to turn frogs into princes.

In the article "What Happened to Effort? Why Students Must Be Part of the Conversation about Learning," author Antonia Lewandowski makes the compelling point that students—particularly high school students—need to be heard on the subject of how and what they learn.[1] According to Lewandowski:

"The current conversation about successful schools and optimal learning is one-sided. Why does student achievement lag so far behind our expectations? If we listen to school board, politicians, government officials, newspaper columnists, and others, we hear strong opinions on what schools and teachers need to do better. But we seldom hear from perhaps the most important group, one that has yet to be seriously challenged to take part in the debate: students themselves."

Lewandowski further makes the point that we are grooming students at all levels to be functioning,

[1] "What Happened to Effort? Why Students Must be Part of the Conversation About Learning," [*Education Week*, December 14, 2005] author Antonia Lewandowski.

successful adults, yet educators and others take full responsibility for their learning. Somewhere along the line, we have bypassed the fact that learning can, at times, be hard work, require effort and development of competence, and students themselves need to be accountable for it.

In an age when public bathrooms have self-flushing toilets and merely approaching the sink causes regulated warm water to flow, responsibility may seem to have taken a back seat. Yet we are the most responsible and the most accountable when we are in charge of our learning, our effort. Guidance and feedback are useful, even crucial, but wanting to succeed because it's ours has no match.

Teachers Learning

Some schools require state or district exams, allowing students several tries, preceded by intensive coaching. I'm reminded of stories about learning that I collected while writing the book *Quality Teaching in a Culture of Coaching*. Teachers also undertake new learning, effort, and hard work to master a certain level of teaching, a new field of study, grade level, or performance improvement. As they do, they receive the attention and the guidance of a coach focused on what the teacher wants—his or her vision of success.

Nowhere is this more important than when a teacher is letting go of total control of learning and allowing his or her students to prevail. It's hard to let go and there is perceived risk in students not achieving what is either mandated or desired of them. In my coaching book there is a true story about two

English teachers at Cranford High School in Cranford, NJ, Barbara Carroll and Karen Bailin. Each had taught more than 25 years. They were in a reciprocal coaching relationship and together came up with a plan to both reduce paperwork and also allow each of them the opportunity to delve deeper into creative teaching.

The issue arose when Karen, being coached by Barbara, wanted to discover a solution to the overwhelming amount of paperwork she had from work with her students: reading three books, developing study or focus questions, grading essays. Letting go of control would take an effort on her part.

Together Barbara and Karen devised a plan whereby the students themselves developed their own focus questions and quizzes, with prior approval by the teacher. Divided into groups, each with its own team of leaders, the students were able to comprehensively delve into all three books during the school year. As Karen guided them and offered additional provocative and innovative points, Barbara observed an exciting and lively interaction among students with learning written all over it. Student-designed quizzes ascertained whether each student in the groups had read the required chapters, and student-led discussions fleshed out the meaning of the books. Essays revealed complete comprehension of the materials. Karen and Barbara not only crawled out from under a mound of paperwork, but felt that the learning on the part of students had never been more pronounced.

Therein lies not only the power of coaching, but the power of empowering students to take responsibility for their learning, for their achievement—to let effort be the engine taking their own train toward its own vision of success. Here's another example.

Earlier we mentioned teacher John Schmitt, who teaches Advanced Placement and Honors Psychology at McDowell High School in Erie, PA. Before he moved to teaching AP and Honors classes, John typically offered his regular psychology students something to motivate them late in the school year. He created a plan he called Option A and introduced it to students at the beginning of the fourth quarter. Option A allowed that students could be exempt from having to take his 100-question comprehensive objective exam if they met certain conditions. The criteria to be met:

1. *Earn an A or a B for the fourth quarter.*

2. *Complete all homework, with no zeros in the grade book.*

3. *Exhibit a positive attitude and participation in the fourth quarter.*

4. *Earn a "C" or better on the "exiting exam"—a required test to earn credit for the school's academic courses.*

5. *Complete a preapproved community service project in the fourth quarter, such as participating in the March of Dimes WalkAmerica, helping with Special Olympics, making a donation to the school blood drive, getting involved with the community, doing community service, etc. that would show knowledge learned in the psych class.*

Students were therefore empowered to take the exam or to take on John's criteria and play into his intent of keeping motivation and momentum going at the end of the school year.

One year he had a fifth-year senior named Andy. Andy only came to school in the morning to retake courses he had failed the previous year. For some reason, Andy also elected to take John's psych course too. This puzzled John, as Andy did not need the course to graduate and, apparently lacking motivation, he failed the first three quarters. When John announced the final exam exemption policy at the start of the fourth quarter, Andy announced he was going to qualify. John thought, "no way!" The student never did homework, rarely passed tests. John challenged him to do it and, what do you know? Empowered by the right to do so and to prove to himself that he could, Andy qualified. He did it.

On a return visit to John's classroom 18 years later, Andy recalled he never forgot the class or the feeling he had of success and accomplishment when he qualified and bypassed that 100-question test.

In *Motivating Students and Teachers in an Era of Standards*, Richard Sagor provides a simple process to assist us in knowing when and how student involvement might occur in the instructional decision-making. He suggests teachers reflect on these questions:[2]

1. *Do I believe there is only one way to accomplish this?*

---

[2] From *Motivating Students and Teachers in an Era of Standards* by Richard Sagor. Copyright © 2003 by Association for Supervision and Curriculum Development. Reprinted by Permission. The Association for Supervision and Curriculum Development is a worldwide community of educators advocating sound policies and sharing best practices to achieve the success of each learner. To learn more, visit ASCD at www.ascd.org.

2. Do I believe there is a best way to accomplish this?

3. Do I believe there are multiple ways to accomplish this objective?

Sagor relates that if he answers Question 1 affirmatively, he feels obligated to teach it that way and shares why with his students. If Question 1 is not affirmative and Question 2 is a Yes, he shares what approach he might use and acknowledges there may be other ways. Then he opens it to students to come up with alternative approaches.

When using this strategy, I don't feel obligated to remain passive. In fact, I feel we do our students a disservice when we don't share our opinions and explain why we favor one approach over another.

If students come up with an approach Sagor feels would not work, he "reluctantly exercises his authority," and shares that he understands their reasoning and has seriously considered it, but has decided on another course of action for their best interests. With an affirmative answer on Question No. 3, Sagor outlines a specific strategy for giving students voice in how they are being taught.

The point is not to hand over the role of teaching to students. Rather, it is to find ways that their effort to achieve can be motivated by their own sense of responsibility and ownership of learning. Students of all ages beam when given something of their own to accomplish. From toddlers to teenagers to teachers and seniors, there is pride and satisfaction when efforts lead to success. It's powerful and it's fun.

Motivators of Effort and Quality

Effort brings about a feeling, an essence of quality. When we are exerting hard work that is meaningful and rewarding—work that results in achieving our vision and our learning—we feel accomplished, useful. Frankly, it feels good. William Glasser, M.D. developed a metaphor that encapsulates quality work in various levels of motivation. Synthesizing substantial research on motivation, Glasser identified a set of feelings and needs that all humans, young or old, relate to. Areas of satisfaction elicit feelings of quality and are therefore motivating.

Glasser's first motivator is **survival**.[3] When people start something new, begin a new project, move to a new town, start a new job, or are faced with new learning for which they must exert effort, even uncomfortable effort, they are motivated to satisfy a need for survival. They came to the new event because it fulfilled a survival need or vision that surfaced, and they are thus motivated to exert the effort to achieve whatever it was they felt they needed in order to improve their abilities.

Once the survival need has been satisfied, the next motivator is a need for **belonging**. People like to belong to organizations; they like to feel useful, in relationship or involved with others. The motivation to succeed is amplified by the need to believe they meet with others' approval. They belong. It feels

---

[3] Glasser's "motivators" on pages 107-111 [summarized] from *The Quality School Teacher* by William Glasser, M.D. Copyright © 1993 by William Glasser, Inc., Joseph Paul Glasser, Alice Joan Glasser and Martin Howard Glasser. Reprinted with permission of HarperCollins Publishers.

good. They are motivated to do more to become even more appreciated or involved with others.

Next Glasser identifies the need for **power**. Here he means a sense of ownership, a sense of being able to accomplish. The power an elementary student feels when he or she has successfully completed all the multiplication functions; the power a team of middle school students feels when it has completed its school science project; power felt by high school students when they are involved with how and where they take a community project; and the power a teacher feels when given the leeway to teach according to his or her own instincts because the teacher really does know how to do it—all these elements satisfy a desire for quality

Right after that is the motivation of **freedom**, probably one of the strongest motivations humans know. There is a sense of freedom in knowing we can succeed, not only with this first effort, but also with subsequent ones. There is freedom in knowing that we are the source of our own thoughts, visions, and beliefs, and can create and recreate them as needed. We are free to achieve success in our own way and our own time with the knowledge that, with our vision, a manageable task, and guidance or support from others, we can do it, over and over again.

Doesn't that sound like fun? That is Glasser's last motivator: **fun**. We do not outgrow our need for fun as we grow older. In fact, the case could be made that that is when we need it the most. Recall kindergarten students coming to school for the first time. Do you think they are motivated to discover each and every toy or book or piece of equipment on a daily basis?

School for them is fun. It motivates them to return. When we have passed by the need for *survival*, the desire for *belonging*, the satisfaction of a job well done and thus *power*; when we recognize we are *free* to learn, teach, create, achieve as we desire, then we are truly having *fun* in life.

With all this at our fingertips, it seems amazing that getting students to exert effort to learn should be so difficult. Perhaps the best practice we can undertake as educators on a daily basis is to step back, enlarge the frame, and look at the big picture. Break down the components of

$$\frac{\text{EFFORT} \times \textit{Ability} + \text{Manageable Task}}{\text{BELIEF} \quad \text{VISION}} = \textbf{SUCCESS!}$$

to see where other motivation and ownership can pop in. Look at how students can be a part of their own learning and where they can be allowed to bring forth their own desire to succeed.

All of this, of course, applies equally to educators, parents, administrators, and adults. We all need to look at the efforts we are expending, the successes we have achieved, and perhaps step back to see where else a little effort can catapult us toward more success, more fulfillment, and more fun. Where do we tap into motivation? How can we create new approaches to our own learning and those of our students that add power, freedom, and fun to the mix?

In our fantasy about the village with the burning grass huts, the natives continued to run back to what they considered their only source of water. They only needed to stop, look, and listen to the flowing resource of water they had in the river that ran right past the burning huts.

Teaching is creating, and thus we have a tremendous resource available to us at all times. Creating a vision for yourself and your students, multiplying ability by moving effort one degree forward at a time leads to success. Add encouragement and an enriched environment that then creates a "wow" and brain-compatible learning. Choose perspectives that serve you, and allow the world itself to provide rich, vital Live-Event Learning. And allow yourself and your students to take ownership, to be empowered to decide, and to act according to the wants and needs that motivate.

There's the river—the flowing, changing, creative resource of power that drives effort and achieves success. Let's dive in!

References

Listed in order of appearance

Foreword

Prensky, M. (2001). *Digital game-based learning.* New York: McGraw Hill. As quoted in Hostetter, O. (2002). Video games—The necessity of incorporating videogames as part of constructivist learning, *Games Research,* http://www.game-research.com/art_games_contructivist.asp

Greenfield, P. M. (1984). Media and the mind of the child: From print to television, video games and computers, Cambridge, MA: Harvard University Press. As quoted in Hostetter, O. (2002). Video games—The necessity of incorporating videogames as part of constructivist learning, *Games Research,* http://www.game-research.com/art_games_contructivist.asp

Hostetter, O. (2002). Video games—The necessity of incorporating videogames as part of constructivist learning, *Games Research,* http://www.game-research.com/art_games_contructivist.asp

Ericcson, K. A., Feltovich, P. J., Hoffman, R. R., Charness, N. eds. (2006) *The Cambridge handbook of expertise and expert performance.* Cambridge, MA: Cambridge University Press. Quoted in Ross, Philip E. (2006). The expert mind. *Scientific American,* August 2006.

Ross, P. E. (2006). The expert mind. *Scientific American,* August 2006, pp. 64-71.

Introduction

Fried, R. L. (2005). *The game of school: Why we all play, how it hurts kids, and what it will take to change it.* San Francisco: Jossey-Bass.

Chapter 1

Parker, S. L. (2005). *212°—the extra degree* (2ⁿᵈ ed.). Dallas, TX: The Walk the Talk Company.

Levinson, J. C. & Langemeier, L. (2004). *Guerrilla wealth: The tactical secrets of the wealthy . . . finally revealed.* New York: Live Out Loud.

Chapter 2

Allen. J. (1979). *As a man thinketh.* Camarillo, CA: DeVorss and Company.

Hill, N. (1963). *Think and grow rich: The Andrew Carnegie formula for money making* (Rev. ed.). New York: Random House.

Singer, B. D. (1974). The future-focused role image. In Toeffler, A, *Learning for tomorrow: The role of the future in education.* New York: Random House.

Kersey, C. (1998). *Unstoppable: 45 powerful stories of perseverance and triumph from people just like you.* Naperville, IL: Sourcebooks.

Sagor, R. (2003). *Motivating students and teachers in an era of standards.* Alexandria, VA: ASCD.

Piper, W. (1930, 1954, 1978) *The little engine that could.* New York: Grosset & Dunlap.

McGinnis, A. (1994). *Power of optimism.* New York: Random House Value Publishing.

Covey, S. R. (2004). *Seven habits of highly successful people* (15ᵗʰ anniversary ed.). New York: The Free Press (Division of Simon and Schuster).

Tyrangiel, J. (2005/2006). Persons of the year: The constant charmer. *Time, 166*(26).

Stephen Levy, Bowman School, 9 Phillip Rd., Lexington, MA 02173 (617-861-2500).

Southern Regional Education Board in Atlanta, GA (404-875-9211, www.sreb.org).

Parachin, V. (2005). Falling forward. *The Toastmaster*, Toastmasters International, August. (story about Florence Chatwick)

Chapter 3

A study of parents and other significant adults of high achieving students. Alachua County Schools, Gainesville, FL in conjunction with The McKnight Foundation; prepared by SRI Perceiver Academies, Inc., Lincoln, Nebraska.

Buckingham, M. & Clifton, D. O. (2001). *Now, discover your strengths.* New York: The Free Press (Division of Simon & Shuster.

Twist, L. (2003). *The soul of money.* New York: W. W. Norton & Company.

Georg, M. (1998). *Purposeful learning through multiple intelligences* [graduate course]. Cadiz, KY: Performance Learning Systems, Inc.

Cooperrider, D., Sorensen, P., Whitney, D., & Yaeger, T., (Eds.) (1999). *Appreciative inquiry: Rethinking human organization toward a positive theory of change.* Champaign, IL: Stipes.

Hammond, S. A., (1998). *The thin book of appreciative inquiry* (2ⁿᵈ ed.). Bend, OR: Thin Book Publishing.

Hasenstab, J. K. (1990). *Questions for life* [system of questioning]. Cadiz, KY: Performance Learning Systems, Inc.

Watkins, J. M. & Mohr, B. J. (2001). *Appreciative inquiry: Change at the speed of imagination.* San Francisco: Jossey-Bass/Pfeiffer Publishing.

Chapter 4

Parker, S. L. (2005). *212°—the extra degree* (2ⁿᵈ ed.). Dallas, TX: The Walk the Talk Company.

Crawford, M. & Dougherty, E. (2003). *Updraft downdraft: Secondary schools in the crosswinds of reform.* Lanham, MD: ScarecrowEducation.

Nater, S. & Gallimore, R. (2005). *You haven't taught until they have learned: John Wooden's teaching principles and practices.* Morgantown, WV: Fitness Information Technology, Inc.

Anspaugh, D. (Director). (1993). *Rudy* [Motion picture]. United States: Sony Pictures.

Moorman, C. (2001). Skywalker sprouts, inc. In *Spirit whisperers: Teachers who nourish a child's spirit.* Merrill, MI: Personal Power Press.

Chapter 5

Fish! Catch the energy, release the potential. (1998). [Motion picture]. Burnsville, MN: ChartHouse International Learning Corporation.

Bridgeland, J. M., Dilulio, J. J. Jr., & Morison, K. B. (2006). *The silent epidemic: Perspectives of high school dropouts.* Executive Summary of March 2006 report developed by Civic Enterprises in association with Peter D. Hart Research Associates for the Bill & Melinda Gates Foundation, http://www.gatesfoundation.org/nr/downloads/ed/TheSilentEpidemic3-06FINAL.pdf.

Cleveland, K. (2006). *Differentiated instruction for today's classroom* [graduate course]. Cadiz, KY: Performance Learning Systems, Inc.

Haggart, W. (1996). *The Kaleidoscope Profile* [a tool to identify learning styles from Performance Learning Systems, Inc. Online and sticker versions for four different audiences]. (800-506-9996, www.plsweb.com/resources/kaleidoscope).

Haggart, W. (2002). *Homework and kids: A parent's guide.* Nevada City, CA: Performance Learning Systems, Inc.

Chapter 6

Barkley, S. G. with Bianco, T. (2005). *Quality teaching in a culture of coaching.* Lanham, MD: ScarecrowEducation.

Byan, R. M. & Deci, E. L. (2000). When rewards compete with nature: The undermining of intrinsic motivation and self-regulation. In C. Sansome & J. M. Harackiewicz (Eds.), *Intrinsic and extrinsic motivation: The search for optimal motivation and performance* (pp. 14-55). San Diego: CA Academic Press.

Kohn, A. (1997). Students don't 'work'—they learn: Our use of workplace metaphors may compromise the essence of schooling, *Education Week.* As first appeared in *Education Week* September 3, 1997.

Noels, K. A., Clement, R., & Pelletier, L. G., (1999). Perceptions of teachers' communicative style and students' intrinsic and extrinsic motivation. *The Modern Language Journal, 83*(1), 23-34.

Parker, S. L. (2005). *212° —the extra degree* (2nd ed.). Dallas, TX: The Walk the Talk Company.

Chapter 7

McGinnis, A. L. (1985), *Bringing out the best in people* (20th anniversary ed.). Minneapolis, MN: Augsburg Fortress Publishers.

Barkley, S. G. with Bianco, T. (2005). *Wow! Adding pizzazz to teaching and learning.* Cadiz, KY: Performance Learning Systems, Inc.

McGinnis, A. (1994). *Power of optimism.* New York: Random House Value Publishing.

Bridgeland, J. M., Dilulio, J. J., Jr., & Morison, K. B. (2006, March). *The silent epidemic: Perspectives of high school dropouts,* Executive Summary of report developed by Civic Enterprises in association with Peter D. Hart Research Associates for the Bill & Melinda Gates Foundation, http://www.gatesfoundation.org/nr/downloads/ed/TheSilentEpidemic3-06FINAL.pdf.

Bianco, T. & Brown, B., (1994, 2005). *Teaching the skills of the 21st century* [graduate course]. Cadiz, KY: Performance Learning Systems, Inc.

Olson, L. (2006) Economic trends push to retool schooling. *Education Week* *25*(28), 1, 20, 22, 24. http://www.edweek.org/ew/articles/2006/03/22/ 28prepare.h25.html?qs=for_every_100_students_who_start&levelId=1000 National Center for High Education Management Systems of Boulder, CO.

Sagor, R. (2003). *Motivating students and teachers in an era of standards.* Alexandria, VA: ASCD.

Parker, S. L. (2005). *212°—the extra degree* (2nd ed.). Dallas, TX: The Walk the Talk Company.

Kohn, A. (1997). Students don't 'work'—they learn: Our use of workplace metaphors may compromise the essence of schooling. As first appeared in *Education Week,* September 3, 1997.

Chapter 8

Kovalik, S. J. & Olson, K. D. (2001) *Exceeding expectations: A user's guide to implementing brain research in the classroom.* Covington, WA: Books for Educators.

Sagor, R. (2003). *Motivating students and teachers in an era of standards,* Alexandria, VA: ASCD.

Jensen, E. (1996). *Completing the puzzle: The brain-compatible approach to learning.* Del Mar, CA: The Brain Store.

Caine, G. & Caine, R. N. (1994). *Making connections: Teaching and the human brain* (Rev. ed.). Alexandria, VA: ASCD.

Harper, M. (2005, December 15). Looking to invest wisely? Ask Farley fifth-graders. *The Paducah Sun, 109*(349).

Hart, L. A. (1998). *Human Brain and Human Learning—Updated,* Covington, WA: Books for Educators.

Bianco, T. (1996). *Discovering the power of live-event learning* [graduate course]. Cadiz, KY: Performance Learning Systems, Inc.

What Kids Can Do, Inc. Voices and Work From the Next Generation; Next Generation Press, P.O. Box 603252, Providence, RI 02906 (Phone/Fax: 401-247-7665, www.kidscando.org)

Chapter 9

Barkley, S. G. with Bianco, T. (2005). *Wow! Adding pizzazz to teaching and learning.* Cadiz, KY: Performance Learning Systems, Inc.

Lewandowski, A. (2005). What happened to effort? Why students must be part of the conversation about learning, *Education Week,* December 14, 2005

Barkley, S. G. with Bianco, T. (2005). *Quality teaching in a culture of coaching.* Lanham, MD: ScarecrowEducation.

Sagor, R. (2003). *Motivating students and teachers in an era of standards.* Alexandria, VA: ASCD.

Glasser, W. (1993) *The quality school teacher.* New York: HarperCollins.

Index

Note:
- Page numbers in italics indicate figures.
- Page numbers followed by *def* indicate definitions.

About the Author

Stephen G. Barkley serves as Executive Vice President of Performance Learning System, Inc. He has 30 years' experience teaching educators and administrators in school districts, state departments, teacher organizations, and institutions of higher education throughout the United States and internationally. A riveting, motivational keynote speaker, trainer, consultant, and facilitator, Steve is known for increasing clients' effort and success by sharing his knowledge and experiences.

You may contact Steve at:
6227 Lower Mountain Road
New Hope, PA 18938
888-424-9700
Fax: 215-862-4884
sbarkley@plsweb.com

Schedule Steve Barkley to speak at your next Professional Development Event!

Steve's keynotes are skill-based with concrete examples and insightful stories, and can be effectively followed by smaller group workshops conducted by Steve and/or additional PLS staff. Steve's topics and titles include:

- *The Magic of Excellent Teaching*
- *Power of Optimism*
- *Teambuilding*
- *Raising Student Expectations*
- *Discovering the Power of Live-Event Learning*™
- *Peer Coaching*
- *Facilitation Skills for Leaders*
- *Leadership for Innovation and Change*
- *Raising Students Expectations*

For more information, or to schedule a keynote or professional development day in your district, call Steve Barkley or Barry Zvolenski at 888-424-9700.

PERFORMANCE
LEARNING SYSTEMS.

More books by Steve Barkley

Steve's books, *Quality Teaching in a Culture of Coaching* and *Wow! Adding Pizzazz to Teaching and Learning* have contributed to teacher and student learning and increased achievement.

Quality Teaching in a Culture of Coaching

This book provides a framework to incorporate a culture of coaching into your own educational environment. You will find concrete examples, a clearly defined coaching process, and multiple resources to build your own coaching program.

WOW!
Adding Pizzazz to Teaching and Learning

Learn how to make school experiences so outstanding that students, parents, and colleagues will say "WOW!" You will find many examples and stories plus tips for WOW lesson plans.

You may purchase Steve's books at:
Performance Learning Systems
72 Lone Oak Drive, Cadiz, KY 42211
800-556-9996 • www.plsweb.com/resources

PERFORMANCE
LEARNING SYSTEMS.